The Dramatic Genius of
CHARLES FULLER

An African American Playwright

MOLEFI KETE ASANTE

W Universal Write Publications LLC

No part of this publication may be reproduced in whole or in part, or stored in a retrieval system, or transmitted in any form or by any means, electronic, mechanical, photocopying, recording or otherwise, without written permission from the publisher, except in the case of newspapers, magazines and websites using quotations embodied in critical essays and reviews.

The Dramatic Genius of Charles Fuller

Copyright © 2015 by Universal Write Publications LLC

All rights reserved.

Charles Fuller/ Molefi Kete Asante
'The right of Molefi Kete Asante to be identified as the author of this Work has been asserted by him/her in accordance with sections 77 and 78 of the Copyright, Designs and Patents Act 1988.'

Book Designer: Author Support

For information:
For information email Rosier@universalwrite.net
Website at www.UniversalWrite.net.
Publisher: Universal Write Publications LLC

Mailing/Submissions
Universal Write Publications LLC
237 Flatbush Avenue, Suite 107
Brooklyn, NY 11217-5224

ISBN: 978-1-942774-01-3

Contents

Acknowledgements . . . . *v*

Chronology with Significant Dates . . . . *vii*

Preface . . . . *ix*

CHAPTER ONE: *The Noble Genius* 1

CHAPTER TWO: *The Artist as Historical Being* 31

CHAPTER THREE: *The Reproduction of History* 55

CHAPTER FOUR: *The Shape of Truth* 73

CHAPTER FIVE: *The Language of Defiance* 101

CHAPTER SIX: *The Theatre of Being Black* 129

Charles Fuller's Works 141

Commentaries on Charles Fuller 143

Charles Fuller's Movie and Television Credits 145

Memorable Cast of A Soldier's Story 147

Endnotes 149

Acknowledgements

African American drama did not come into being with the advent of Charles Fuller's writings, but it made its mark on the literary establishment with Fuller's contributions. In many ways the acknowledgements that are necessary for this manuscript are also an on-going project.

Ed Smith, director, producer, and actor, really pulled me out of my comfortable den with the burning wood fires in Buffalo, New York, to thrust me into the seats of small theatres to see the work of leading African American playwrights. I owe a debt to him and to the many playwrights that made the cold winters of Buffalo much warmer. They would have names like Ed Bullins, August Wilson, Lorraine Hansberry, Amiri Baraka, Ntozake Shange, Pearl Cleage, Anna Deavere Smith, Alice Childress, and James Baldwin, and later Lynn Nottage and Suzan-Lori Parks would inspire me.

I was chair of the Communication Department at SUNY-Buffalo during the 1970s and early 1980s and Ed Smith stood at the center of our thriving art community. So by the time I got to Philadelphia and found myself engaging with John Allen and the Freedom Theatre I had grown deeper in my understanding of theatre. I applaud Sekai Tillman Zankel who was actor, writer, and dynamic manager of the Department of African American Studies when I became head of that program. Charles Fuller was on our staff and I read the manuscript of the book by Nilgun Anadolu-Okur that featured him, Larry Neal, and Amiri Baraka. I send out acknowledgements to Nilgun. However, this book could not have been published without the support of Charles Fuller himself. We talked for hours and hours in every corner of Philadelphia. I am truly blessed to have had my ideas contradicted, disputed or confirmed in our conversations.

While several publishers were interested in this book with changes I was unable to make, I am very happy for my publisher, Denise Rosier, who is also a great editor and friend for finding worth in the volume as it was written. I was interested in the intellectual contributions of an important African American thinker to the field of drama; this is what UWP saw as well and I want to acknowledge the support that the company has given to my work.

Molefi Kete Asante

Chronology with Significant Dates

1939	Charles H. Fuller is born in Philadelphia, Pennsylvania on March 5th.
1959-1962	U.S. Army in Japan and Korea 1962
1965–1967	La Salle University
1967	Co-founded with Larry Neal the Afro-American Arts Theatre Philadelphia
1969	*The Village: A Party*
1975	*The Brownsville Raid*
1980	Won an Obie Award for *Zooman and the Sign*
1982	*A Soldier's Play* wins the Pulitzer Prize
1982	Fuller receives Doctor of Fine Arts degrees from Villanova University, LaSalle University, Chestnut Hill College
1984	*A Soldier's Story* is a successful movie, screenplay nominated for an Academy Award A Golden Globe Award, a Writers Guild of America Award and an Edgar Award.
2010	*Snatch: The Adventures of David and Me,* becomes his first published novel

PREFACE

Charles Fuller is not a simple writer; he may be the most complicated African American playwright of his era because of his attention to literary style and ordinary values as well as his devotion to the ethics of human interaction. Indeed, as Fuller's major plays indicate, he is certainly an authentic voice of the American stage due to his nuanced assault on the substantial racial matter that occupies American reality. The more one reads Charles Fuller the greater the passion one has about his intellectual orientation, his genius as a writer and his strong natural sense of justice. From the late Sixties when he was writing regularly for the *Liberator* with short stories and essays that captured life in North Philadelphia to his writing of the novel *Snatch: Adventures of David and Me* in Old New York, Fuller has been displaying his quest for a human community that is balanced, enlightened, and progressive.

I met Charles Fuller first through his plays and then through the *International Herald Tribune* when I lived in Zimbabwe. In the *International Herald Tribune*, a paper Americans tend to read overseas, Fuller was interviewed about his writing style, and identity, a subject that seems to always come up with black writers. As is his character Fuller was straightforward in his answers, clearly embracing his most genuine self and revealing for his readers his innermost thinking about society. The story revealed little about his drama, but a lot about his personality and temperament. At the time as the first African American scholar in the free Zimbabwe I did not know that I would later write a book about Fuller since I was there actually to lead the first diploma program in communication and media for the Zimbabwe Institute for Mass Communication under a Fulbright grant. However, I was struck by the affirmation that I felt when I read Fuller's robust defense of himself as a black writer. "I was black before I was a writer," struck me as the words of an authentic person situated in the center of his own historical experiences. This, for me, was a writer who was sane, intelligent, and committed to dramatizing the stories that meant something important for the lives of the masses.

This was a significant achievement in a society that creates disconnects between the standard portrayal of reality and ordinary experiences. A black person who lives in the United States is compelled to handle a number of contradictory relationships with the state, the local government, the overarching techno-structural realities of institutions and belief systems, and the hypocrisy of the keepers of the founding documents. How you keep sane in the midst of so much chaos is through mental discipline and a tough stance towards one's own sense of self. Fuller is an exceptionally proud man who knows that it is possible to create art and to remain attached to the reality of social experiences.

Later I would come to know Fuller's influence on younger writers and I would see how his unassuming brilliance would be instructive to other playwrights. His plays are structurally elegant yet clear and clean in the execution. This is because one knows that the works have been studied, the characters molded like clay and firmed up like solid stones when they are set on the stage. They are not loose, damp, or dangling, but sturdy, mature, and shaped personalities with a lot of possibilities. If Fuller seems to catch anything it is the sense of history in his works. His moods, nuances, and temptations tend to be toward honesty and justice; there are no false moments in Fuller's plays. I think it is important to say this because some readers or viewers of his works may find elements that are unfamiliar but these particular turns in the plays have rootedness in African American history and culture. Fuller is different in this regard than August Wilson who used much more of the ritual, mystical element of the culture to capture his audiences' imagination. Fuller, on the other hand, uses plot, character, and structure in such a manner that the reader is led to the source of the dramatic truth almost against will.

While the characters are strong in Fuller's plays they are not predictable because the writer holds in his hand the keys to their ultimate action and almost at every turn Fuller throws the reader or the spectator a bone to pick and then takes it and runs in another direction as if to say, "now you know, now you don't." I think it is fair to say that Charles Fuller humanized the African American drama by announcing that we were mature enough as a nation to accept all the vagaries of living in a complex racial democracy. Simply put, there was nothing that was known to human beings that was not known to black people.

Some may be tempted to accuse a writer of portraying only one particular side of a human issue, but no writer can be expected to cover all possibilities of human attitudes and behaviors. The best one can say is that the drama of a dramatist defines the boundaries of that writer's interests at that time. In my judgment the condition of the writer himself, his emotions, interests, ambitions, intentions, loves, dislikes, curses, and joys, taken collectively, represents the substance of the drama. Fuller is not a one-dimensional human and hence he is not a one-dimensional writer. One cannot come to maturity with a body of experiences richly augmented by the experiences of his childhood friend, Larry Neal, and others who lived the streets of Philadelphia when everyone seemed to be *totin'* and not have a special angle on, for example, character construction. Fuller once told me that he found lots of his characters in the lives of the people he grew up with in North Philadelphia. "All you had to do was to go outside and walk to the corner store, and life would be right in front of you, active, dynamic, intrusive, and sometimes risky," he said.

No one can accuse Fuller of not flowing in the sense that flowing is the ability of a writer to move with the situation, the tide of chance, the rivulets of opinions, and the tributaries that feed the emotions and attitudes of a writer deeply engaged in the conditions of his society. Whatever else one might want to say about the environment of this writer from a literary perspective the truth of the matter is that he is one of the most consciously historical writers of his time. Nothing escapes Fuller that needs to be in the play. There is a meticulousness that might annoy the average reader but it indicates that serious work in the form of vetting ideas and characters has been done to create a whole image that remains with the audience.

CHAPTER ONE

The Noble Genius

Charles Fuller remains one of the most imitated dramatists of the American stage and heir to the greatest tradition of African American playwrights. His nobility as a writer is derived from his character as a person. He is unspent, creative in a way that causes those around him to seek his counsel, and this is the beginning of nobility. The career of Charles Fuller has played out on some stage over a long period of time. He came of age when the world was coming out of the insecurities and instabilities of the Second World War; the anxieties of the Korean Action; and the protests against the unpopular Vietnam War. Fuller felt the rising tide of conservatism in the American society at the same time as he participated in the more aggressive demands of black Americans for justice and he used these themes as fuel for imagination and genius. It is out of this cauldron that Fuller examines the nature of the wars in human hearts and between humans; he is clearly dedicated to the task of setting straight the crooked paths. His dramatic imagination is enlivened by his persistence in explaining or better yet dramatizing the moment when disorientation becomes orientation, when the unclear becomes clear, when the vulgar becomes the respected. Late capitalist consumer culture has had little to offer to Charles Fuller because he has retained the desire to challenge the narrow *identitarian* restraints that command most attention when it comes to black ideals and yet he is one of the most authentically black writers of his era.

In my judgment Charles Fuller's dramatic power clearly derives from his convergence with technological America in a sort of Ogunic fashion of creative genius and the evolution of African humanity. This gives him an edge on a globally connected drama; that is, African American drama finds in Fuller an advocate for a universal appreciation of human sameness. Fuller's *globality* rises in his concentration of the subjects that he knows most about from the military to modern art, from community life to capitalism, but he is never far from the racial hypocrisy of his own nation. Charles Fuller is an interdisciplinary, multidimensional character in the play of his life, searching for the core values that emerge in the diverse experiences of human beings. He has been honored and is still being honored by societies, clubs, organizations, universities, museums, and institutes around the country and yet he remains one of the most serious students of the human condition in contemporary literature. Fuller is impeccably precise in his writings and this has meant that those who honor him and call him a genius must read his works or else they do not know what they are talking about. In an era of branding Charles Fuller is the titular head of the consistent art worker seeking to make a difference in our categorical assumptions without chasing the neonic and digital hounds of publicity.

Charles H. Fuller, Jr., was born in Philadelphia, Pennsylvania, on March 5, 1939 to Charles H. Fuller, Sr. and Lillian Anderson. He was educated at Roman Catholic High School, LaSalle University, and Villanova University. Later in 1982, after he had won the Pulitzer Prize, Fuller received the DFA from LaSalle, Villanova, and Chestnut Hill College. In 1959 he joined the United States Army and served in Japan and Korea. When he completed his service in the army he went to LaSalle University in 1965-1967. During 1967 he co-founded with Herb Showell the Afro-American Arts Theatre in Philadelphia. In the late 1960s he teamed with his lifelong friend Larry Neal as Philadelphia's dynamic duo in the arts. Neal left for New York to work for the *Liberator Magazine*.

Fuller's father was a printer during a period when few blacks held jobs as printers. Fuller Sr. was an industrious and capable entrepreneur who believed that books, newspapers, and magazines were not mere commodities to be sold but held the best thinking of a community. Fuller's mother, Lillian, was a voracious reader and housewife who encouraged her children, Charles, two sisters and a younger brother, to read by often saying "Most of what you need to know can be found in books." In addition to their natural children, Charles Sr. and Lillian also raised twenty foster children, seventeen were African Americans, and three were Puerto Ricans, for nearly twenty years. Encouraging all of their children to learn how to read; be diligent in their homework assignments, and to learn to write well, became part of the daily work of Fuller's parents. Thus, both his mother and father's vision influenced Charles Fuller, Jr. and this may be the reason he has maintained a lifelong interest in publishing, writing, editing, and reading.

Fuller is essentially an urban compatriot. He is completely engaged with modernity and postmodernity in the deepest aspects of seeing the world from the perspective of science and technology as a part of writing and reading. Yet he declines the fluidity and lack of place often found in the work of postmodern theorists. Fuller's engagement is with urban diversity as it tackles issues of race, class, gender, and culture; these are the urban elements that make him a fully engaged city man. He finds in the practical elements of writing generally and drama specifically the components that drive any comprehensive city person. One could not dream of Fuller as an agrarian because what he is all about is the close encounter of humans with each other.

My reading and locating of Fuller's work, of course, stems from an Afrocentric perspective that views Fuller's corpus from the standpoint of seeking African agency in all subject places. Fuller provides the student of literature as well as the student of history with a large textured fabric from which to draw conclusions. I want to transcend the idealist notion that sees Fuller's work as simply brilliantly conceived forms or neutral shapes of culture or words without politics. This is not to say that there are no idealist possibilities in a theoretical review of Fuller's works; that would be far from the truth. Rather I am insisting that alongside any idealist conceptualization of the writings of this artist there must also be the fact that Fuller is deeply political. Indeed, it may be that he is one of the most serious political dramatists we have had in the past fifty years. I have discovered that his dramatic interest and themes are found in the severe historical epoch in which he immersed himself. Because there is no bombast in his person or in his writings he has found his reflective time uncompromising and richly endowed with acres of wisdom.

The Black Revolution of the 1960s was Fuller's launching platform.[1] This movement became the plinth of many of his ideas; it even grew his consciousness. Fuller was a part of the process of creating art and drama regardless of the Established Order in Philadelphia. With his friend and compatriot Larry Neal and musician Jimmy Stewart he challenged the artistic institutions in the black community by setting up venues for more revolutionary and transformative art.[2] Rarely were the works of these artists exhibited, for example, at Freedom Theater the home of most black drama in Philadelphia during this period. Yet the fire in the words of Charles Fuller and Larry Neal contributed to the New Black Arts Movement that stoked the ambers burning in a thousands cities and towns across America.[3] It could be argued that Philadelphia as much as Newark, New Jersey, with Amiri Baraka, and Brooklyn, with Ed Bullins, was the source of much of the dramatic energy of the movement. Fuller and Bullins became friends after Bullins' son was killed by municipal negligence and Fuller wrote a letter to the *Philadelphia Inquirer* demanding that the city take responsibility and pay the Bullins family for their loss.

Most revolutions are simultaneously challenges to the order and acceptance of a new order. The new order for Fuller and Neal would ultimately lead Fuller to New York and the Negro Ensemble Company; Neal, after an incredibly creative life of action, would have an untimely death after being shot in New York in l981. Without revolutionaries, however, there would not have been a Black Arts Movement, and Neal and Fuller were both engaged in serious dialogue with their generation.

The objective conditions of black life did not change by virtue of the Black Arts Movement. The poverty, fear, disintegration of the commercial sectors, disease, lack of adequate housing, and poor schooling remained the same during the early days of the movement. What changed overnight was the consciousness of the artist who dared to claim his autonomy and with it the authority to assert new ways of seeing the objective reality of black life. This change in the artist and other artists and the masses of the people would be the only effective remedy for the stagnation of ideas and actions seen in the oppressed. Fuller, like most of the writers of the 1960s and 1970s, was baptized in the sacred waters sprinkled by the Harlem Renaissance. The impact of those Harlem writers had not waned when Fuller and Neal began their careers. The complex set of beliefs, attitudes, and rhetoric that made political and social action necessary and possible during the era of Civil Rights, Black Power, and Black Arts Movement, came with numerous attendants in every artistic and social field. Black scholars in communication, political science, sociology, and social work defined themselves as activist scholars committed to equality and justice in order to differentiate themselves from the so-called "mainstream" of their fields. As in the social sciences and the humanities the professionals in the arts as well as the lay artists in the black community rushed to create new avenues toward transformation. The position of this new black activist scholar or activist-intellectual or as the artist Maya Asante says, *artivist,* was radically different from that which was claimed in the earlier era.[4] What the Black Revolution, as it was called, showed was that the white Establishment was contestable because it was not, as it had been perceived by blacks, monolithic and all-powerful in its doctrine of white supremacy. There were whites that understood the idea that community development was in their best interest as well. Thus, when blacks involved in the struggle for justice in law, housing, employment, and the arts questioned the provincial attitudes that kept issues from being discussed or presented they essentially joined the social revolution. Of course, the revolution tore down the tradition of white exclusivity and erected a new tradition in its place, one based upon black agency and ultimately multicultural respect. It was clear that whites were not the only people who could create and activate ideas; other people were now fully engaged in the process of creation. In a religious metaphor, sacrilege is transformed into the sacred, that is, the old becomes new, but simultaneously new and moving in a trajectory of the traditional.

No critical writer can afford not to interrogate the larger context of a subject like Charles Fuller and therefore I will examine the inter-texuality of Fuller's works to demonstrate that there is a larger narrative into which his works fit snugly but I will also extract the originality from this context to name and identify what I see as the genius of Charles Fuller. No writer sits as an iconic atom, unique in construction, totally apart from the community that made him. Fuller's richness is derived from the thickness of African American culture, his experiences in and outside of that culture, and his special reading of literary and historical texts and personal narratives.

We can easily convince ourselves today that we can see something that Fuller saw when he began to write. Perhaps this is so, but most likely we are looking with hindsight at the achievements of his art and the art of others that make it possible for us to imagine worlds that were impossible for some people. The best writers are really ones who stretch our minds and expose us to new possibilities. This path, of course, is fraught with the perils of criticism but once reflection takes place the brilliance of the idea is often seen and we recover a sense of the prophetic nature of the best dramatic art.

Charles Fuller became astute at an early age in negotiating the territories that were his in the city of Philadelphia because he was a student of history and a participant in the urban community during the time of the gang and mafia wars. Philadelphia, like New York, Chicago, Los Angeles, and scores of smaller cities had its own internal dynamics to gang power, authority, and control in the 1940s and 1950s. There were named gangs who controlled areas of North Philadelphia, West Philadelphia, and South Philadelphia. One did not want to be caught outside of the comforts and conveniences of one's own community at the height of gang violence. There were elements of the Crips and the Black Mafia in Philadelphia as there was other, sometimes, less well known gangs. Actually in Philadelphia gang members usually operated by blocks since the city is tightly organized around blocks and blocks of row houses. Meanwhile the police in the 24th and 25th districts in North Philadelphia appeared to be the most active against gang violence, though the entire inner city area, on all sides, South, West, Southwest, North, and Germantown, were familiar to Charles Fuller. He would later become a housing inspector, a role that would send him into the most unbelievable dank, dingy halls of musty darkness he had ever seen. This was a chastising role for Fuller because he would experience things that he had never seen, conditions of children that had never crossed his mind, and the incredibly bad manners of adults toward children and children toward adults. Here in the inner chambers of domestic housing Charles Fuller would come to learn that humans, blacks and whites and Latinos, could perform some of the most heinous crimes known to humans. In these houses he would find child abuse, heroin addiction, and later crack use, and filth, but also he would find love, passion for life, hope for the future, and decency. Everything was human. He was always a writer and this would of course become substance for his plays.

The Pursuit of the Human

In the strictest sense of the word Charles Fuller is an intellectual, not merely someone who writes but someone who reflects on the entire process of bringing into existence new ideas. Thinking outside of the box could have been invented by him because his parents taught him that things are not always as they seem. He knew this from his early childhood and became involved in the drama of ordinary lives from listening to the provocative conversations that took place in his house when he was still a young man. Fuller sought to create an art form that would allow African Americans to respond to every challenge as ordinary human beings who achieve extraordinary levels of understanding, empathy, and power, noting always that African Americans had to confront the existential problems of being black humans.[5] Four years in the United States Army in Japan and Korea taught him about the complexities of human relationships and the contingencies of military life. More than that, however, was the fact that issues around petty dislikes and brute racism paled in the face of life and death in combat on the battlefield.

Fuller found his way from the army to Villanova University. He remained for a few semesters and then left to pursue more literary objectives. Soon he entered LaSalle University in Philadelphia and after a few semesters he leaves LaSalle as well, seeking to improve his writing skills. Two years after leaving LaSalle University he received critical mention for his play, *The Village: A Party*. This play introduced the controversial tension between mixed race couples and drew the critics to the profound reflective manner of Fuller's mind. Fuller was quite busy during the early 1970s writing plays that would be mounted by the Henry Street Settlement Theatre and the Negro Ensemble Company in New York.[6] As had become his mission Fuller took on the writing of another powerful drama exemplifying the complexity of black life. He often used his military experience to probe the mind of African Americans in the army. *The Brownsville Raid*, an 1975 play, dealt with the struggle between black and white civilians in 1906. When the dust had settled on the Brownsville Raid an entire black regiment had been discharged dishonorably from the United States Army. Tensions would last into the late 20th century over this incident until 1976 when the soldiers were pardoned. Fuller knew that the black soldiers had found themselves, like other blacks, in an absurd world that they did not create. They had landed in Brownsville, just as they had come from Montgomery or from Cleveland, second class citizens in an insane world created by men and women who were not just ignorant but obscene in their hatred of blacks. Fuller delved into this play with skill, posing human questions, and demonstrating a deft pen that gave voice to the combined thoughts, attitudes, and aspirations of black people. Setting a pattern for some of his later drama, Fuller, obviously impacted by his years in the army, found the military to be a rich source for the gritty realities of African American life. Thus, it is easy to see how Fuller spans African American history from the 1906 Brownsville Raid in Texas to the 1940s army base in *A Soldier's Play* in Louisiana. From the pedestal of history in the 1940s, a military moment, Fuller organizes all of the pieces of a puzzle that are to be put together in contemporary and future times. There is the notion that he is talking about today although we know the setting is the American South in the 1940s on a segregated military base.

What a stellar history the dramatist had to draw upon. At

the very beginning of the American nation black men had distinguished themselves on both sides of the conflict between the American patriots and the British loyalists. Fighting for their liberation was always the motivation for the Africans who gave their energy and frequently their lives in wars. The War of 1812 had seen black sailors create the conditions for victory in several skirmishes on the Great Lakes. The Civil War itself involved 186,000 African soldiers, many trained at Camp William Penn in LaMott, Pennsylvania, a few miles from where Charles Fuller was born. Certainly Fuller knew about the Buffalo Soldiers because some still lived in Philadelphia during his youth. They were old by the 1950s and 1960s and often talked of their bittersweet glories years before. These old Buffalo Soldiers knew that the fight against the indigenous people was not their fight and yet many of them or their older comrades had gone to the Southwestern United States to chase the Chiricahua-Chokonen Apache leader Cochise and the Bedonkohe Apache priest Geronimo Goyaale because this was a way to support their families after the Civil War. Old heads who could do nothing else or who did not want to farm anymore found the army the place to be.

Fuller knew these stories and the narratives of black heroic actions at San Juan Hill in Cuba. Theodore Roosevelt had lauded praise on the African American troops who fought to drive the Spanish out of Cuba. In fact, African Americans were fond of quoting Brigadier-General J. C. Gilmore when he wrote in 1898 glowingly that the black troops were "fighting and storming works as infantry, ... having shared equally in the heroism as well as the sacrifices, ... now voluntarily engaged in nursing yellow-fever patients and burying the dead." More recently, Fuller had knowledge of the bravery of the Tuskegee Airmen and the numerous examples from World War II, the Korean War and the Vietnam War. Fuller wrote a play about African American airmen during his years in California in the 1990s. The play was never produced but is a part of Fuller's quiver of plays. To write one had to be prepared to write and the fundamental path to preparation is knowledge. This is precisely why Fuller spent many hours reading on military tactics, organization, life, and culture.

Fuller would accumulate accolades for the realistic style of his writing and the remarkable depth of his dramatic work. In 1980 he won the Obie Award for *Zooman and the Sign*, which was produced by the Negro Ensemble Company, and directed by Douglas Ward Turner. The play was a spectacular examination of how easy humans can resort to violence and how willing humans are to demand justice if they have been wronged. In *Zooman and the Sign* a Philadelphia teenager kills a young girl outside of her house. The neighbors are baffled and afraid at first but soon are provoked to collective anger when the girl's father places a sign outside the house. Although Fuller does an exceptional job showing how Zooman is a product of the society he also strongly suggests that the society has the capacity to produce justice. The play has a currency that has made it a standard of the college theatre circuit. It is also popular with community theatres.

Fuller returns to the military with *A Soldier's Play* that tells the story of intra-black tensions within the larger context of a racially charged Southern society.[7] I will return to this play throughout the book because I believe in many ways it is one of the best dramatic model we have had of the existential realities of black life. Fuller puts the issues fully in front of us and we are made to know that revolution, if it is to be a real revolution, must consider the complexities of what it means to be black in the United States. Generations of artists and thinkers have shown that this is no easy task; today it is even more complicated by a renewed emphasis on diversity and mixture.

In *A Soldier's Play*, a black officer, Captain Richard Davenport, searches for the murderer of a black sergeant on a Louisiana army base in 1944. The tragic hero, Sergeant Vernon C. Waters, is portrayed as one seeking to save the black race. Prior to his death Waters says, "They still hate you." The assumption might be that the murderer has to be white; after all this is a racist society and the killing of black men, especially black soldiers in uniform was not unheard of in the South. However, Fuller launches into the psychology of intra-black relationships, honor, shame, expectations, self-hatred, and pride in order to eventually solve the murder. This play had the longest run in New York of any of Fuller's plays. Directed by the indefatigable Douglas Ward Turner at the

Negro Ensemble Company the play was critically acclaimed as a masterpiece and he received the prestigious Pulitzer Prize for Drama in 1982.

Charles Gordone had received the award for *No Place to be Somebody* in 1970. August Wilson would be awarded the prize for *Fences* in 1987 and *The Piano Lesson* in 1990. Suzan-Lori Parks would receive the Pulitzer for her play *Topdog/Underdog* in 2002. Later in 2009 Lynn Nottage would receive the same prize for "Ruined." However, in many respects Fuller was the first African American playwright to formally claim an African identity upon receiving the award. Gordone appeared to have a complex racial identity that tugged at him for most of his life; thus he claimed to be Irish, Native American, French, and "part Negro." Nevertheless, his experiences as a waiter in New York gave him the material for his first play. It was a heated polemic about race and it won for him the Pulitzer. Of course, Charles Fuller acknowledged Gordone but found him out of the mainstream of African American writers who were both artists and committed to telling a full African American dramatic narrative. When August Wilson, a fellow Pennsylvanian, received the Pulitzer for *Fences* he was to become the second clearly committed and racially conscious African American dramatist to win the prize.

Consider the fact that Fuller's play combines history and the military, two of his major themes. Yet the play is broad in its reach, colored with imagery, myths, sports, superstition, legacies, and traditions found in the black community. Fuller once told me that he is interested in everything and one sees in his response to nature, illustrative materials from street dialogue, heroic experiences during the gang war days of sectional and sectarian Philadelphia, and we see his response to the environmental and structural inequalities in the society. If any writer knows the power of inspiration in everything from Roman Catholicism to Black Nationalism, from physics to political détente, Fuller knows. Fuller has never been able to point to one thing, one fact, to one facet, one touch that inspired him because everything does. This does not mean that he leads a life of chaos; it really means that he is disciplined, using everything that comes his way as a lesson to be refined, meditated over, and then employed in a dramatic work. *A Soldier's Play*, for example, carries a theme that emanates from Fuller's fascination with the military and African American history yet he uses his intelligence, experiences, and understanding of human beings to develop deep characters that are attached to ideas. In the play when the black non-commissioned officer named Vernon Waters is murdered at Fort Neal in April 1944, Captain Richard Davenport, a black lawyer of the 353rd Police Corps Unit, arrives at the base intent on finding out who murdered Waters. Davenport's character is the narrator in the play and through his various interviews with soldiers we began to see the dramatic context in which the murder happened. The soldiers are attached to Company B in the 221st Chemical Smoke Generating Company. Thus, Fuller places the locus of the action in an all-black segregated camp in Louisiana during the height of World War II. What is so spectacular about the penetrating examination of black self-hatred that is illustrated by the relationship between Private C.J. Memphis and Tech/Sergeant Waters, who are both dead at the beginning of the play, is the direct relevance that this play has to oppression and its concomitant evils in the contemporary lives of African Americans. It is a universal problem that Fuller tackles because in many respects it is the intersectional issue with all oppressed groups who believe that the best way to convince the oppressor that you are not inferior is to demonstrate that you are just like the oppressor. For examples, Waters is obsessed with the idea that blacks are no different than whites. His disparagement of African culture is a telling sign of his self-hatred; he despises every instance that reminds him of blackness. In fact, he believed that by acting white himself he could show the men around him how to act white and therefore be equal to the whites. C.J., a brother with an easygoing humorous personality laden with superstitions, proverbs, music, dance, and the kind of joy of life that Water loathes as a negative stereotype that needs to be abandoned or expunged, is right in his face, always loving who he is.

In this play Charles Fuller has given us the most authentic African American portrayal of the military in modern times. *A Soldier's Play* is written with a forceful tension between the words and actions of the characters that possess the most primordial myths of the African American community. These characters are not unknown to America and they are certainly not unfamiliar to blacks. We live with them each day and we have come to see their mythological forms as parts of our cultural experiences. Of course, the play heightens the traits and perhaps distorts some of the habits but in the end we are on taken into the inner sanctum of our souls. Situated in a segregated army camp in the South during World War II, a group of black soldiers play out the complex relationships of segregated life and behavior with a stunning, terribly chilling honesty that creates a cathartic release in the audience. Fuller' play is classic because it combines all of the proper elements of the black culture from the disdain that is felt by some toward others, the inferiority complex that dogs the minds of some of the soldiers and the concrete, meaningful, and powerful responses that emanate when the search for the murderer of Sgt. Vernon Waters, is discovered. When the play went from the stage to the silver screen as *A Soldier's Story* it carried with it the progressive pursuit of two values, truth and justice, and in the process of discovering both it brought us almost, as personally as the stage play, to a confrontation with ourselves.

This is why one could say that the search for the murderer was secondary to the delicate search for black roles and responsibilities to each other in a segregated society. One remembers the poignant words of Sgt. Waters, "They still hate you!" Captain Davenport is the key protagonist in the story. He is skilled, talented, efficient, and knowledgeable. Given his task he must operate with objectivity and care; he must be thorough and uncompromising. Of course, there is obstruction all around because of the intent of a black man to discover the truth. Whites did not want the truth discovered because it could easily have been a white murderer given the overpowering evidence of murder of black men and women all around the state of Louisiana. They knew, as well as the blacks, that the murderer would turn out to be white, who else kills black people in the South? While some critics felt that this should have been the conclusion of the play the brilliance of Fuller is to take us almost across the river in the boat of familiarity and then to tell us that we have to swim the rest of the way to the shore. Furthermore, the fact that Fuller has the Captain examine every detail, disposing of all leads, and concentrating on the truth provides us with a masterful denouement. Davenport is able to find the murderer and the reason for the fratricide.

I am a fan of the irony, humor, and entertainment value of this play. Yes, this is entertainment in the most real manner because it allows us to experience all of the emotions available to a situation such as this one. I see the play or the movie and realize that the artist has pulled on every emotion that I can possibly experience in one dramatic production. I am sad, I am proud, I am angry, I am happy, I am disappointed, and I am shocked. The greatest bit of irony however may be the fact that the soldiers were happy to be going to war to fight the Germans. Perhaps there is something in human beings that suggest a reason to prove themselves when there is tragedy, disillusionment, and the exposure of their own fragility. War provides the opportunity for "real" humans to show that they are not afraid and that they are not cowards. The irony, of course, is that these soldiers were determined to show that they were the equals of any other men by entering the war. In effect, changing the situation to one of engagement with the enemy could alter Waters' thought that the camp situation was boring.

Fuller demonstrates his ability to handle contradictions with the deftness of a commanding officer. Black life gives the writer an enormous amount of dynamic contradictions and one can see tension between the various social and political positions held by black people. The fratricide that emerges in black life is dealt with by Fuller as dramatic material because the essence of drama is conflict and nothing is more purely conflict than constant fratricide. In *A Soldier's Story* Fuller stacks the cards so clearly, deliberately, that we are brought face to face with ourselves and catharsis will have to be occur. The playwright forces the characters to confront their own suicidal and fratricidal demons just as he would force whites to abandon their rabid racism. This is the meaning of Fuller's character building.

Despite the seemingly centrality of conflict in the play, Fuller also demonstrates the reality of the social context. Not only is conflict present it is present within the context of the lived experiences of the soldiers. Using what I believe was a strong African cultural line of thinking Fuller shows us the problem of the present condition of the men by linking them to a contextual tradition. In this regard he generously identifies the genuine from the adulterated in a repeatedly brilliant manner that can be demonstrated through his use of negotiation, point and counterpoint and strategic dislocation.

Fuller is able to pack into the situation, the soldiers in the camp, all of the radicalism and many of the attitudes of the African American Movement over a generation. He sees the negation, rejection, and discrimination of blacks as being a part of the entire corpus of African American response; in other words, they are parts of the same resistance. Of course, it is not just resistance that we see in the dialogue and characters of the black soldiers but transformation. Perhaps we could even imagine that at some point in the future, perhaps even because of the war some of these black soldiers will experience a re-Africanization that will save their souls. The writer knows that the soldiers must guard against co-optation but he does not tell us everything that he knows. This is left to our imagination. Enough has been done in *A Soldier's Play* to let us know that dislocation can sit at the door of all discourse around culture, identity and consciousness. I am not sure that Fuller intended to discuss the polarity between racial rigidity and the fluidity of identity yet some will read into the play a commentary on who is black. Is the black person the one who has one drop of African blood or is identity so fluid as to be able to defy identification? Or is the black person the one who maintains the purest sense of justice?

There is no question that the election of Barack Obama may have finally made the last line in the play, "You'll have to get used to Black people being in charge," acceptable or at least tolerable to many people. It is this line that was most criticized by some who feared black assertiveness. Not only did Barack Obama become president in 2008; he did it while retaining his African surname, thus putting a lie to those who felt threatened by African names as a damper on their careers. The highest job in the land went to a man with an African name.

Fuller wrote the screen adaptation for the movie, *A Soldier's Story*, in 1984. For his work he was nominated for an Academy Award, a Golden Globe Award, and a Writers Guild of America Award, and his screenplay won the Edgar Alan Poe Award establishing him as a brilliant writer of dialogue and direction for movies and television.

Charles Fuller is not just a major writer; he is a transformative writer whose works continue to influence other major writers such as Lynn Nottage, who in the style of Fuller, seeks to engage the audience with the profoundly human actions of each of us. We are not freaks; we are human with all of the capacity of other humans. Fuller has written numerous plays, some of them with military themes, such as the "We" series and others that deal with the fundamental decisions that humans must make everyday. He has written movies for television and in 2010 a novel, *Snatch: The Adventures of David and Me in Old NewYork*, for young adults. His aim has always been to transform society through the power of his reality-based writing. For his genius as a writer he has amassed scores of awards besides the Pulitzer and Edgar Allen Poe, such as the Guggenheim, Rockefeller, State of New York and National Endowment for the Arts awards. He remains a member of the Writers Guild of America East, the Dramatist Guild, and continues to exercise his prerogatives as a Pulitzer Prize Winner in helping to choose other candidates and awardees. Furthermore, he is active in the African American community as an interpreter of the artistic contributions being made by younger artists. Fuller is a professional writer in the sense that he identifies as a working writer in several genres. This is important because it allows him to demonstrate to those younger writers who seek to make a living as writers that it is still possible to hold to one's views and make an artistic impact. To say that Fuller is a professional writer is to say nothing more than the fact that he embraces his own freedom to create as a part of his mission. He is the master of his tools, not merely the owner of them, and therefore his style, language, nuances of emotions, and actions are at the level of an artistic and professional imperative. One must freely write out of a sense of necessity. In this way we are able to see both freedom and necessity as parts of the same creative process. To paraphrase Jean-Paul Sartre, drama does not serve the writer's freedom; it demands it.

Fuller's plays, set in the fluid milieu of a socially ambivalent America, grasps the necessity of artistic freedom but also demonstrates the powerful magnetic attraction of racial and communal conflict even when it is appropriately held at bay in the background of a play. This one sees in both *Zooman and the Sign* and *A Soldier's Play* because in the foreground the principal actors are black and yet in the background to both of these famous plays the racial issue stalks the boundaries of the audiences' sensibilities. The dramatist's freedom is singular but it is not disconnected from the freedom of the audience. The interplay between what the dramatist writes and what the actors perform and what the spectators see establishes a useful platform of mutual freedom. Here each participant plays a role in the creation of good drama. It always begins with good writing and this is where Fuller sets up his shop.

An Angle of Philosophical Light

Charles Fuller is one of the most philosophical writers of his generation.[8] He is attuned to the profound emotions of ordinary people and he brings the widest possible brush and the most authentic personal engagement with words to his writing. In effect, he is the intellectual's artist, committed to getting right the most powerful attitudes and thinking in the community as a barometer of humanity. While he may have been brought to drama by seeing a Yiddish play it was after directing the Afro-American Arts Theatre in Philadelphia and writing and directing "Black Experience" for WIP radio that endeared him to his home audiences. Fuller emerged as the favorite dramatic son of a large Philadelphia's artistic tradition which has included the likes of John Coltrane, Sonia Sanchez, Grover Washington, Patti LaBelle, Larry Neal, Marian Anderson, Paul Robeson, and Ed Bullins, just to name a few.

Probably since Fuller's Pulitzer Prize in 1982 he has been known simply as the Master Playwright, but he is in fact a comprehensive and multi-talented literary genius. His early writings included poetry, essays, and short stories. An acute ability to hear dialogue and to sense conflict propelled him into drama. Charles Fuller created skits, sometimes from his short stories, and one-act plays and then full-length dramas. In 2010 he published the novel *Snatch: The Adventures of David and Me in Old New York* for young people. It is a powerful and suspense-filled narrative created around two brothers in colonial New York. Here perhaps is Fuller's keenest demonstration of his gift for character, plot, action, suspense, and metaphor within a historical context.

Charles Fuller demonstrates the multi-dimensional literary personality of the greatest writers in the African American tradition. He challenges the anticipated outcomes in the lives of everyday African Americans and thereby projects in his brilliant writing the most human example of our lives. As the second African American playwright to receive the Pulitzer Prize for Drama, Charles Fuller solidified his place in the literary pantheon in which he continues to shine brightly.

Fuller's work is current and remains vibrant and meaningful to the historical and social understanding of our society, but it is more than that because it focuses us on eternal, that is, recurrent situations and responses. Fuller is a weaver of a fabric for eternity without the showmanship of self-righteousness. If he writes with passion, he does not think of it as passionate. If he does not write with passion, he does not believe that it is without passionate elements. This is not a paradox. I say this because my reading of his dramatic works has always featured a quest for gathering kernels of truths that transcend the current condition of his characters. Who are they to become when the play ends? Who and what am I to become when the curtain closes?

We cannot divorce his plays from space and time. For example, Fuller is writing in the 1980s and the play, *A Soldier's Play*, is set in the 1940s and the influences on the writer are found in everything prior to the production of the play. Rebellion had been in the air and Americans were moving toward a convergence of ideas regarding race as a social construct at the same time as Fuller was writing about the complexity of a racial epistemic. Who is to say that a black cannot kill a black? This was an underlying question in the face of the most murderous assault on black men in urban areas, an assault carried out not by the KKK but by other black men. If one lived in Philadelphia, Chicago, New York, Atlanta, Baltimore, Detroit, and Washington, one was aware of the awesome melancholic narratives of the death of blacks by blacks. Yet there was something raw, revealing, and unsettling to those who found it impossible for blacks to murder when they read *A Soldier's Play*.

Drama is not only catharsis, but also an arena for growth. Being involved in the daily, ordinary lives that we all live, brings us to a particular location in the process of social maturity. It is not that we live outside of ourselves or outside of our conditions but rather that we are engaged in the recreation of ourselves each day by transcending obstacles, prohibitions, and barriers that seek to prevent our maturity. Fuller's stance, as seen in his most iconic writings, is that human beings can rise above the social conditions and establish an ontological response to all forms of oppression.[9]

Fuller prefers reason to ego. In reason he finds the eternal drama that resides in the interstices of time. And what is the meaning of a character in time if it is not a character for eternity? I see the questions posed and answered, not in a declaration or proposition but in the positioning of dialogue and character in the interplay of the dramatic work; that is where Fuller shows his reason and reasons. He seems to ask, "How can I truly capture the self-conscious yearning for entertainment without the quest for eternity?" It makes me ask, "Has this society with so much tragedy turned only now to Tyler Perry's comedy?" Has it always been such a place where the true condition of African people was invisible and the glazing over suffering, ignorance, and cultural death allowed both blacks and whites pleasures like those of the burned brutalities, and dangling bodies from oak trees? Are we truly in a new world or merely the residents of the old one, awakened and frightened? Perhaps this is why Fuller's original ending of the play *Zooman and the Sign* makes better sense to me than the ending in the movie. In the play we discover that the sociopath is also a victim of the society like the little girl he killed. In the movie we are made to witness street justice in a cold and calculating manner meted out to the sociopath.

What sickness befalls our communities when little girls or boys are shot sitting on their porches? Who is responsible for this breakage of the cosmic unity? I am reminded that the ancient Africans in Egypt believed that the per-aa, pharaoh in Hebrew, was the consummate cement for human society. If the per-aa is weakness in the littlest bit he puts the entire cosmic order at risk; when the per-aa is well then the society blossoms and flourishes as if the entire heavens open up to the community. All activities that we consider to be tragic have within them the possibilities of wellness. Humans are the responsible agents to make the proper choices that will benefit the collective society. We live neither in a dream nor a nightmare, but in constant action where decisions are made in a Sartrean sense. Decision, in effect, is the reality of our lives.

If we are awakened as a community, do we act to overcome the nihilism that stares us in the face as a result of the oppressive and destructive situations that we experience? Fuller's dramatic work is reflective of his optimism that human beings can do better not because we are gods but precisely because we are human. What humans do humans can do and what humans are capable of anywhere on the earth, other humans can attain the same status. Equality if it is to be meaningful must reach into all dimensions of our social and moral lives and provide us with that angle of philosophical light that Fuller so passionately searches for in his writings.

Fuller does not appear to have a particular epic condition of black America in mind when he writes his plays. I say this because there are no heroic examples that he seems to enjoy more than others. In effect, his drama is a critique of society and if there are winners and losers they are the *arrogants* of power, the shakedown artists of destiny, and the perpetual victims of bad choices. The *arrogants*, those who tend to know everything and seem to know everything, are the puffed up egos that we find in almost every circumstance where blacks are asserting dignity and nobility. In the end, the good people of the world will abide by the traditions that have established our most abiding values of justice, love, character, mercy, respect, and fairness.

CHAPTER TWO

The Artist as Historical Being

There is a contradiction, no, perhaps a paradox in Charles Fuller, not unlike the juxtaposition of reality and idealism, the authentic and the inauthentic, or the real and the unreal, faced by all black people in America. He is a black person who lives in the United States of America; that is one of the strangest and most difficult contradictions on earth. What possibilities would have existed for a Fuller in a society without a history of the enslavement? But Fuller understands this paradox and creates out of it, fusing together the parts of our experiences, contradictions and misgivings, with our hopes and desires in a way that resolves our most critical issues. We have perhaps not taken enough notice in the literature, the dramatic essays, and critical reports of this ability of the artist to bring characters to a translucence that reveals everything. When you write about an artist, seeking to delve into his secrets, you often discover that the secrets are hidden in plain sight. I mean when I wanted to know how Charles Fuller would resolve the contradiction of place, just being in America, I had to examine what he achieved in his plays. For example, *The Brownsville Raid* gave Fuller the opportunity to demonstrate his historical knowledge as well as his dramatic brilliance, but as a critic I sought out the intricate avenues of meaning and the intimate facts emerging from the Brownsville tragedy itself. While I concluded that the achievement of the writer was stunning given the reality of racial discourse or the lack of rational racial discourse on the Brownsville incident I also felt that the author's historical sensibility showed him to be equally aware of four themes: the *military, race, moral choices*, and *drama*.

The age of Fuller may be called one of the most military of all ages. He was born in the middle of the greatest conflagration that had ever befallen the world, the Hitlerian rampage of Europe that plummeted the world's industrial nations into the dragnet of misery; he came of age and found his adolescence during the Korean War; and he became an adult as a soldier in the Vietnam War era. But the reason I refer to his age as a military age is not to appeal to hyperbole but to distinguish Fuller's period, for example, from that of other great writers whose work may have occurred between the great wars, the First International European War and the Second International European War, normally and euphemistically called World War I and World War II. Of course, one could argue that the American nation has rarely been without some military intervention in some part of the world. A recent analysis has demonstrated that there has never been more than ten years of absolute peace in the history of the United States since 1900. At some point, then, it is necessary to see the impact and the results of this martial spirit as contributive to the age of Fuller. The writer is a creature of his environment perhaps more than any of us because he imbibes the elements of the social and political air that he breathes as he imagines what the world could be like with or without this or that. Charles Fuller is personally a very peaceful and friendly man but to say that he is affected by the wars that he has seen, by his own internal struggles, and the battles on the streets of urban America is only to emphasize his humanity.

War is the ultimate drama because in war one is confronted constantly with vulnerability and death, with insanity and chaos, and with fear and guilt. Fuller learned that war and the ramifications of war, murder, hubris, arrogance, shame, and courage, were the calling cards of human commonality and therein was the source of much of the drama in the world. Being in the military and serving his country gave Fuller a personal angle on the tragedy and comedy of human frailty. Yet it is his collective sense of identity with a larger field of humanity that brings him to the citadel that allows him to survey the banalities of human beings at war with themselves and their communities.

Discourses and drama around race did not catch Charles Fuller by surprise; as an African American in Philadelphia he grew up in the center of the racial storm in the nation. Like many young people of his generation Fuller was baptized by the alliance of African independent movements that had direct influences on the United States movement and the rise of Black Power as a salient and critical element in the struggle against racism. Like some cauldron shaken by a giant the mixture of youthful exuberance, nationalism in Africa and among black Americans, and an atmosphere of the possibility that all scourges of the earth could be defeated, became the most instructive of all pedagogical moments for the young writer. Race was clearly at the forefront in Africa and the United States. Richard Wright had written *Black Power* in 1954 and James Baldwin had followed ten years later with *The Fire Next Time*, one dealing mainly with Africa and the other writing about race in the United States. African people were throwing off the shackles of years of colonialism and African Americans were shaking loose the fears of taught inferiority. As the discussion of race and racism took on more urgent terms Charles Fuller joined the fray with his own literary gifts. There was no question in his mind that he had to deal with his own political, social and racial reality as a writer. How could he avoid the most compelling discourse of his time? Yet he was an artist, the best type of artist, one who understood that art, if it were to be effective and lasting, had to consider the most profound issues of life. Fuller's work would be universal in its appeal but it would definitely have local relevance in its reality. I see in him the attitude of an enlightened writer who molds bits and pieces of human experiences into one magnificent quilt of circumstances and possibilities. There are no definite solutions in the best art although there are always conclusions. When one delves into the ditch of race and the impact of even the discussion of race on human beings one is likely to discover the most unusual reactions.

One can say that moral choices, or better yet, ethical issues were at the center of Fuller's concerns in war and race. Who is to be charged with criminal actions? What political motivations promoted discrimination and prejudice? What role had to be taken by Martin Luther King's "good people" in order for justice to prevail? How could a man filled with the passions of the ancient priests of the temples of Waset or the Muses, Thalia and Melpomene, humor and tragedy, or the more accessible spirit of action that one sees in modern dramatic presentations use his social and political energy to redress the inequities that he sees in society? Of course, Charles Fuller would have no part in the crass use of drama as political liturgy; his understanding of the art form of drama is rooted in the 20th century and he is heir to the dramatists who believed that it was possible to show in performances the emotions, attitudes, and possibilities of human nature. This is his real contribution to the form. I do not consider it comedy or tragedy or any other form than the pure actionable statement of human frailties it is. Since racism, especially as presented in our era as white supremacy, sits at the entrance to American society with outstretched hands asking for pittance from any newcomer Fuller appears to have a desire to educate in order to have audiences refuse to pay for any inequities or injustices, regardless to the race of the persons involved. Chekhov, Zola, Miller are known for their dramatic works but their challenges could not have been any more complex, difficult, and far-reaching as those confronted by Charles Fuller and other African American writers whose intellectual and dramatic personas were activated by both internal and external societal factors. They had to deal with white supremacy in the imagination of audiences, black and white, and the internalization of memories that had colored the prism through which they saw the future. In addition, they were fully engaged with the particular problems of their characters that, like the writers, had to deal with the complications of racism in their own environments.

Zooman and the Sign was an extraordinary example of the challenges for the writer. Charles Fuller had to know through experience intellectually and emotionally the type of society that created the conditions for his characters. Furthermore, he had to struggle with his own emotions as he saw the enormity of the choices that had to be made by characters. Who is to say that the characters had it easy in their lives? Or how could a young black man go so horribly wrong in a society that boasts about its quality, exceptionalism, and abundance of opportunity? Fuller drew upon his urban experience, his work as a housing inspector, and his intensive readings in sociology to complete the play *Zooman and the Sign*. Without this background Fuller would have found the play impossible to complete with all of the incredible nuances of community and individualism.

When the off-Broadway production of *Zooman and the Sign* ended its 2009 run on April 26th of that year, it had recreated the expectant air of brilliance. I saw the play in 2009 but I had read it many times and felt that some of its aspects were autobiographical in the sense that the writer knew firsthand some of the situations he was describing. This is not necessarily something novel since most playwrights attempt to use what they know as a part of their dialogue, discourse, and drama. However, in Fuller's writings the autobiographical part is not just in firsthand accounts, but also in his mission to advance human equality. There is no unattainable uniqueness because we share human capabilities and therefore we all have the same possibilities for attaining uniqueness. Since drama tends to be autobiographical even if only in the sense that the writer can only produce out of his or her own collection of myths, tales, experiences, and ideas, then the authentic writer is on a quest to know himself.

What is autobiography anyway? It is dialogue with context, a discourse on one's life with the activities of our experiences tucked into descriptive nodes about who we are and what we have become. In the case of Charles Fuller, we do not have a self consciously written autobiography but we have enough materials in his plays to assess how he has dialogued with his experiences and the public history. Furthermore, we have the larger inscription of a domain encircling Fuller's history and literary production and from that situation we are able to draw political and cultural inferences about the work by mediating between what is written and what is unwritten on the page, though found everywhere else in the society. Like any good writer Charles Fuller's eyes and ears have been opened always to the events that surround him, those that preceded him, and the possibilities of those that will come after him. I do think it is impossible to be a good writer without cultural vigilance; this has to be one of the hallmarks of the genius in African American drama.

John Coltrane, the famous jazz musician, looked for articulations of culture and spirit everywhere and anywhere he could find it; the same could be said about the way Fuller approaches his own writing. He is no mystic, however, and will not be seen pursuing Hindu, Christian, Jewish, Islamic or Buddhist philosophies, yet he enthrones a sort of rationalism with his humanism that allows him to be opened to knowledge from all corners of the world. Fuller's cultural vigilance is not ethnocentric in the sense that he valorizes the African idiom above others; however he is wired to appreciate the intricacies of the southern African American culture which is a part of his family's heritage as much as the urban environment. Nevertheless, he has learned from all cultures and speaks the language of humanity through specific expressions and allusions of African American culture.

> ***Wilkie***: *Worked harder and faster than everybody—-wasn' a man on the team didn't like him. Sarge took to him the first time he saw him. "Wilkie," he says.*
>
> ***Wilkie and Waters*** *(simultaneously): What have we got here?*
>
> ***Waters***: *A guitar-playin' man! Boy, you eva' heard of Blind Willie Reynolds? Son House? Henry Sims?*

Fuller pulls Blind Willie Reynolds from Louisiana or Arkansas and puts him in the dialogue. Reynolds in real life had been blinded by a shotgun blast to the face in the 1920s and by the time of the play in the 1940s Blind Willie was on a roll as a Blues singer. Son House was a legendary singer who made his first recording with Paramount Records in 1930. Henry Sims was about ten years older than Blind Willie Reynolds and Son House and had established himself as an accompanist with Charles Patton in the 1920s. Sims served in World War I as a soldier in France. So when Fuller has Waters speak about Blues giants he is demonstrating a profoundly iconic symbol of African Americans at the same time he is showing a universal appreciation for culture.

Fuller's life is private, but he is public; I mean you will not be able to gain any information about him from the self promotion of a new age guru type announcement nor will you ever see Fuller projecting himself as this incredibly gifted writer, although in my judgment, he is truly one of America's best dramatists. Where you will find him is in his dramatic writings for stage and television. In some ways he is like the old *babalawo*, Yoruba priest, who was teaching a group of people about the Odu Ifa when a young man raised his hand to question him. "How is it that you have all of these people listening to you, even following you, if it is not because they are sheep? If someone with a strong mind heard you they would not do everything you asked them to do." When he had finished speaking the *babalawo* said to him, "Sir, come up here on this stage with me." The man left his seat and came to the stage. The *babalawo* said to him, "Stand over here to the right of me." The man went to his right. But then the *babalawo* said to him, "No, I think it is better if the audience see you stand on my left. So please, sir, stand on the left of me." The questioner then moved to the left of the babalawo. It could be surmised that the questioner thought that the *babalawo* was giving him this position so that he would be able to speak to the audience, but this was not the case. When the man had settled in his position on the left of the *babalawo,* the wise man said to him, "Now see, you have come to the stage as I have asked, you have moved to my right and my left as I have asked, what is the difference between you and the people you characterize as listening to me. You have also listened and obeyed." And so it is with the subtlety of Fuller's genius, we act, move, and obey without ever knowing that the context between the artist and the reality is seamless.

Charles Fuller is a dramatic teacher as well as an instructive dramatist; indeed he is an exceptional teacher, capable of presenting the strongest truths in ways that the learner, audience, gets the message even when they do not know they have gotten the message. There is no attempt to strike you in the head although when you have seen the play and reflected on it you may think that you have been hit on the head. In this way Fuller is like our *babalawo* who writes or speaks in such a way that the mission is almost like a stealth machine; one does not know that the blow, whatever its character, has been delivered. This is the message of great drama.

Charles Fuller in many ways epitomizes someone born of the warrior era in America. To characterize Fuller as a child of such an American era is not to be far off the mark. After all he was born a mere six months before Adolf Hitler's German Army opened the most horrendous war in history by invading Poland. During that September the world was shocked by the sudden, unanticipated military awe produced by Germany. By the evening of September 3, 1939, Britain and France had declared war on Germany, and within a week other countries like New Zealand and Australia, had joined the fray. Other nations in the British Commonwealth supported Great Britain in its war against the Germans. Six bloody years of ferocious fighting plunged the world into an orgy of bloodletting that would stand as the high water mark for military engagement. More nations had been involved, more territory had been fought over, and more lives had been destroyed than ever in history. One can say that from the broad boulevards of Warsaw to the orchards of Normandy, the snowy slopes of Norway to the heat throbbing deserts of Libya and Egypt, the insect habitats of the jungles of Burma to the coral reefs of the Pacific, from London's towers to the Japanese gardens of the East, guns and bombs were heard and nearly every major political power became involved in the struggle. Sixty million people lost their lives through a combination of war, poverty, brutality, and the holocaust during the early life of Charles Fuller. He does not escape this history and neither does he insist on escaping it. There is nothing more engaging about Fuller than his remembrances of soldiers. He is a soldier, a pan –African nationalist who counts time from the wars, and it does not matter which war since it is the martial culture, the spirit of liberation and freedom that drives him toward self determination. Fuller's ability is quiet, not loud; you will not see an exuberance that floods the banks of reason in him. A warrior with a MacBook Pro can mow down thousands of enemies with a single sitting. But there is also this internationalist soul in Fuller that positions him as a global citizen weaving drama that curves around mountains of difference and into the valleys of similarities. Part of this similarity is the fact that to be born in America at a time of war or the rumor of war is to be just like 90 percent of all Americans, a people who has never had long period of international or national peace. One has to count Fuller among the most solid producers of this ancient genre because to engage his work is to encounter a blazing field of combat for the nature of society. Frank Rich had it correct when he wrote in the *New York Times* that "Mr. Fuller demands that his black characters find the courage to break their suicidal, fratricidal cycle— just as he demands that whites end the injustices that have locked his black characters into a nightmare."[1]

What Fuller recognizes is the oppressive modality of fear and he seeks to eradicate that by suggesting courage as an answer to the fratricide within the black community. No earlier black dramatist had raised the question or sought an answer to the question so directly in this vein; therefore, none could propose a solution. However, the reality of need, that is, the necessity to prevent the absolute murder of black men by black men, as one example, is preeminent in the mind of a reasonable writer. There is a serious issue of black fratricide when other black men have killed more black men since 1970 than were ever killed by the Ku Klux Klan. For the black community the prospect of re-gaining a sense of place, an authentic reaction to time and space, means that we will have overcome the need to kill each other when we have discovered our own transparency as human beings. Fuller knows that this is highly unlikely and that the best thing that we can do is to find the courage to confront the evil that stares us in the face.

Thus, the homogenizing of the dramatist's plots takes the path of unifying the lessons of our common humanity. Fuller's plays tend toward the merging of our ideas in radical and transformative ways. Here we are able to see how he creates the speaking voice that becomes the standard of the black world that is a reasonably important voice in the world at large.

THE SPEAKING VOICE

A dramatist inherits much of his voice, if he is a good listener, from the mode of speaking and listening that emerges from his community. Fuller's immediate communities are North Philadelphia and South Philadelphia, two areas of the urban North where he grew up. Yet he is the product of a Georgia family resettled in Philadelphia and the sounds of his language are the sounds of the South.[2] The voice of Fuller is an optimistic voice like the voices of his people so full of the hope unborn. In the sounds of the city Fuller hears the reverberations of thousands of conversations and he is able to convince his readers that these voices are alive, talking points and counterpoints in the backyards, basements, corner stores, barbershops, and beauty parlors of the community. . Yet he brings his own special curvature to the long line of tradition inherent in being a cultured person within the context of other people who speak and listen like he does. Thus, Fuller's style and to some degree, form, can be said to be chosen from rhetorical and social possibilities found in African American culture and the larger American social context. Of course, we know that the particular signature of style is the dramatist's own. To say this is to merely claim the author's freedom. I mean we sometime believe that a writer should be forced by politics, religion, or his or her parents' dreams to write something other than what he or she writes, but in the end it is freedom to be someone that really counts.

To be concerned with the assessment of a speaking voice, an authorial voice, about human life is to be convinced that words matter and that disciplined and correct words are necessary for the advancement of society. Fuller's central point helps us to understand why a writer could write with such passion about his times, and other times, during war and establish a platform for future writers. He is an artist speaking out of his own voice but engaged with the creation of a process for self-criticism. Charles Fuller reveals new forms of personhood in that we see him grow as a person and as an author into a representative human being with emotion, ethics, and style. His dramatic texts have helped us to construct a serious audit of the author. One knows something about all authors by disclosing the secrets of their words and actions in their dramatic works. Fuller is no different as an author who uses words precisely and with the deftness of a genius that listens to the language of his community.

Fuller's works reveal an intense dance toward immortality as seen in his expectations for the characters he creates for us. We are able, on the other hand, to see how the artist meets our expectations. Charles Fuller has spoken enough and written enough that we know essentially what he says he believes. His artistic inclination has always been to allow his characters to tell the stories that he finds most daunting, appealing, puzzling, and contradictory. He does not see life in a simple manner and knows that in most instances of human conflict there is more to the story than meets the eye upon first seeing it. This is the intriguing aspect about his art; it seeks the puzzle, in James Baldwin's words, the conundrum of life and then he lifts it to an even greater height. Elevating the bond between history and reality, however, is a part of the intrigue in Fuller's drama because his own bond to the same history and reality irrevocably captures him, humanizes him, and liberalizes him.

It is impossible to learn from Fuller's writings without some appreciation of the social and political context. There can be no understanding of Fuller's character development, plot construction, or ultimate philosophical statement in a vacuum. There has to be an approach to generative creativity in the milieu of political action in order to rescue the texts from obscure and quixotic interpretations. The odd look into the drama of time and power allows the reader to engage the ambiance of Fuller's drama.

I like to focus on the fact that Fuller's rise to prominence as a literary presence came to the front because of his ability to translate the oral traditions and styles of African Americans into a more literate and powerful expressive tool on the stage. Fuller's sensibility is refined, deep, and authentic. His characters buzz with both the orality of the traditions and the immediacy of the moment. I think that the generative nature of his prose reflects his poetic side. He has both a poetic and a historical sense, the best combination for a dramatic writer, and it is in this convergence that produces the creative result we see on the stage. Fuller's awareness of the national contradictions when it comes to injustice and justice, to promise and despair, is key in the transformation of this philosophical and mythical base of knowledge to drama. One is not held hostage to time and history; in Fuller's case, he uses the weapons at his disposal to enter the room of literary expression with audacity. Who would have thought at the time that a writer would use the most entrenched institution, the military, to highlight the racial dilemmas in the American society?

The American military is the most sacrosanct of all American institutions.[3] At the very foundation of the nation the military under George Washington was thrust into the front of the American imagination. Stories of brave men, and a few women, became the grist of the mill of public understanding about the necessity for the military. Establishment of academies that trained soldiers, pilots, and sailors was meant to cement the power and the influence of the military in the lives of ordinary people. Children of the working classes went to the military services or to the military academies to learn discipline, respect for authority, and protection of the nation. Fuller takes on this powerful institution in a nuanced way. He knows it as a multidimensional organization with powerful transformative capabilities at the same time it is the site and agency of various types of violence.

In my search for the artist's voice I explored the class dimension to Fuller's work just to see if perhaps there were other aspects of his drama that I had missed. My own suspicions, based on readings of his work, were that he was determined to highlight the use of race as an American concern and to demonstrate that the African in dealing with the racist structure of the society could overcome it with his own will to humanity. Of course, I know that the relationship between the oppressor and the oppressed, the capitalist and the worker, the whites and the blacks, is constrained by economic factors as well. Yet in the history of the African American the impact of class was less important than race. The historical pathology caused by the doctrine of white racial domination distorted class distinctions and made race the most salient characteristic in a discussion of race and racism in this society. Fuller knows that whatever is considered bad, whatever is despised, and whatever is thought to be inferior tends to be designated as being black. Fanon had said it in the 1960s and it had been repeated many times since numerous writers identified the term black with negativity and evil. The Manichean allegory of black and white where black is evil and white is good sat at the center of America's race problems. Those who see intelligence and emotion, savagery and culture, subject and object, as part of the structure of racial knowledge, understand immediately the attraction of Fuller's intellectual ideas. The absolute negation of the humanity of Africans by white racial supremacists, for example, results in a counter negation that allows one to question the humanity of whites. This is the meaning of Fuller's characterization of the issues in *A Soldier's Play*. It is possible that those who see the plays of Fuller, especially if they are racists, will come away being both repelled and attracted by the human portrayal of Africans. In effect, the African American is no different in drives, emotions, capabilities, and fallacies, than any other American. On one hand, a spectator may be attracted by this but also repelled by what a human being, being black, is capable of doing, even to another black!

Feelings are important in all drama; the negation of the terms of blackness and humanity are both emotional and irrational. The fact that the racists would deny the black person the capability of violence while seeking to hold onto the possibility that whites could but blacks could not is to protect violence as some type of sacred icon. On the other hand, the black person who is determined to demonstrate that only whites commit murder against blacks is living in the same irrational world. In a society where the murder of black men is more likely to occur at the hands of another black man than a white man it is irrational to assume that blacks could not or would not kill another black person. This was a fact as true in the 1940s as it is now at the top of the 21st century.

Charles Fuller's philosophical accent emphasizes complexity and each of his characters arrives at the moment of action with baggage, of course, the more human the baggage the more profound and less trite must be the conclusion of the action. I mean it would have been quite trite for Fuller to make the killer in *A Soldier's Play* a white man. Here you have African American soldiers in a southern community where whites during that era did not appreciate blacks wearing United States military uniforms. The record of black soldiers being killed in their military uniforms throughout the South is one more example of the sordid history of race in the United States. So, yes, of course, Fuller could easily have made the murderer in his drama a white man. This would have been suspected and even expected in some circles but we would never have felt the same emotions, experienced the complexity of our own being, or resolved to participate in the universal drama of human redemption had he done so.

Fuller's drama, like his prose, is often dialectical and can be understood in terms of what appears as the opposite. His realism must be seen in light of the romantic idealism portrayed by some other writers. This is the core of Fuller's brilliance. The dramatic narrative of *Zooman* must be read in terms of the society's own destructive impact on African American youth. Who is the real enemy of the black community? One answers the question while not negating the fact that we are all responsible for our own actions. Fuller's extraordinary concern with safety speaks to the lack of security experienced by the African American community. It is a drive for public safety but also an intense passion in his work for the secure place, the location of harmony, the space for reading and writing and making and doing and living and loving; this literary and political motive helps to keep back the chaos that comes with insecurity. In effect, the enemy then is chaos, racial, social, and psychological and anything the dramatist can say to steer his audience toward a brighter future makes peace with internal questioning. I think it is clear that Fuller understands that mere integration of the races or expressions of civil rights cannot re-make the wholeness of the African person because the conditions, the actual experiences of the horror of our lives in America, have changed our own perceptions of ourselves as Africans. Our ethical and moral principles have been twisted by the horrors, poverty, self-hatred, and *mini-violences* that have resulted in the breakdown of fraternal feelings inside many black communities. Far from transcending these conditions because of knowledge and education, we have often descended into the same chaos that we have tried to avoid and Fuller, in a strong contemporary sense, extends our humanity by conceptualizing and dramatizing the African as nothing more or less than human. I am not suggesting that Fuller is a theorist of this transformation; he is a playwright who has come to the conclusion that something is lacking, missing, absent in the realization of African humanity. Our means of self-comprehension and self-determination, in the Afrocentrist's sense, must mean a re-commitment to the idea of common purpose and common mission. This is the essence of the challenge of identity.

Two elements comprise identity; they are *biology* and *culture*.[4] A playwright who is able to convey the tension between biology and culture in the constancy of conflict will always be seen as pioneering. In this sense, Fuller is a pioneer in search of identity. Now I do not find this a postcolonial or postmodern anomaly because Fuller's interest is not essentialism in the fundamental sense but rather a belief that there are certain values and heritages we share with a community of people. He would be among the first to abhor the idea of an unchanging cultural referent, yet he knows from experience that to make the plays that he makes he must dip into the fertile womb of an agreed upon set of symbols, however changing and changeable.

Of course identity itself can be compromised by the very search for it. I mean, if one has no clue then the search can be amiss. In Fuller's case the world of gods and heroes may be different but the world of humans is the same. We live in the same cosmos, the same universe, and we are cut from the same stone. Our sense of destiny and justice may not depend on how we are victimized simply by our *hubris* but rather by the combination of that hubris with the failure of *maat*.[5] This is an African concept and I have chosen to display Fuller's particular quest in the tradition of Africa rather than merely rely upon the common Greek ideas. The reason for this is clear when one understands the condition and the mythic quest of Africans to bring about liberation from destruction, anomie, and nihilism. Fuller is not just a playwright; he is a playwright who finds the dramatic idiom necessary for his quest to better us.

The transgressions of *hubris* are certainly critical in the dramatic form; the Greeks saw these transgressions as fundamental. Thus, we confront Ajax's envy, Achilles' anger and Agamemnon's pride as crimes or sins par excellence, but alas, when it comes to the situation of the African in the United States or any other Western nation made by the aberrations of human enslavement, the conditions must be extended to include other transgressions. Fuller recognizes the *maatic* claim on order, balance, harmony, justice, righteousness, truth, and reciprocity, (concepts identified as consistent with *maat* by Maulana Karenga, the authority on this subject), as a warrant for communal reconstruction or response. Here we are again in the realm of identity, that is, an identity that questions the entire scope of the political and social situation that defines black America. How do we hold back chaos in such a situation? What projection of art can intervene in the process of anarchy?

The dramatic act of society is a historical interaction between *hubris* and *maat* because it occurs in the moment of our decisions. On one hand the individual's response to his or her condition is critical to the overall good of the society and may be seen as a part of the cosmic wellbeing. Yet on the other hand, the society or the governing band of the society, the Establishment, in the language of the 1960s, the white Establishment to be more precise, is also responsible for the condition of the characters in *Zooman, A Sol-*

dier's Play, *the Brownsville Raid*, and so forth. We are gathered in a congregation of commonality and no one escapes the individual or common problem; we are victims and victimizers. This is the profound reality of Fuller's drama.

CHAPTER THREE

The Reproduction of History

Charles Fuller is a dramatist with a keen sense of history not a historian who writes plays. There is a difference that goes to the core of the dramatist's art that becomes the structure of forms, the presentation of myths, old and new, and the stylized evocation of realism or idealism on stage. The real issue here is whether or not history can be reproduced at all; I mean what is it that the historically minded playwright does anyway? Is it history or a re-telling of history, or myth? History has its own pursuits and vices, but they are not so detrimental as the *not-telling* of history. Malcolm X said that history was best suited to reward our studies, but this does not tell us what the dramatist does. What is it that Fuller is getting at when he concentrates on the historical events in our lives? One might ask in a different vein, "Does the playwright concentrate on history anyway?"

The answer might take the form of questioning a system of ideas that projects history as false or projects a false history. How can an African American dramatist, bent on making a transformation, overturn a system in which he participates? There is no fatal weakness in any answer to this question but what we see in Fuller's drama is a form of critique of the very community from which he emerges as a dramatist. Thus, he makes abundant use of the dramatic idiom.

Consciousness of history does not announce itself; humans must create the consciousness of history. What I see in Fuller's plays is the creation of regions of consciousness where we are able to extract our own experiences. One can then critique his or her relationship to the external world based on a knowledge of history. The problem with drama based on history is that one must know something about the history in order to make sense out of the external facts. How one feels is another issue altogether. Of course, one can say that I could capture the essence of the *Brownsville Raid* without knowing the factual story but no one could deny that knowing the facts would make me a better, more informed spectator of the play. It is like viewing the opening or closing ceremony at the London Olympic Games and not having any appreciation for the history of the United Kingdom. You could catch the artistic and aesthetic elements without truly understanding the myths, meanings, and metaphors of the events. Satisfaction often comes in small doses. One does not have to be an Oxford or Cambridge graduate to appreciate all of the elements of the producer's phenomenal ceremonies. However, I would say that one would have to know something, to have experienced something, and perhaps to know and experience something to make more sense out of the production than a superficial liking or disliking. I mean it is possible to like and enjoy something on one level only to find that there are more intense and intricate parts to the drama.

Theater's power, originality, and vigor stem from the mastery of certain traditions without which theater is limp, vapid, and ineffective. Charles Fuller has captured two of the principal dimensions of the African American tradition. He knows the vast wealth of African American legends, folktales, and narratives as a legacy of his many nights of reading and he became a student of African American history at an early age. Combining these two elements, the fictional and the historical, are central to Fuller's ability to carry out good dramatic writing. Fuller's ideal spectator is a person who has a richly textured intellectual background. He abhors the lack of information that some spectators bring to the dramatic audience. Intellectual penury leads to dramatic embarrassment in the sense that the littlest idea, nuance, or metaphor might be missed in the play and hence the meaning of the passage lost to the reader or spectator. A spectator who is not careful with the background of a play is a prime candidate for the drama of propaganda. If one does not know, then anyone can say anything and gain adherence; this is after all the essence of propaganda. However, the good dramatist is one who appreciates the community and seeks to enlighten it without embarrassment. One can say that this is dramatist-spectator mutuality since both are seeking success and neither wants to be accused of failure.

Fuller's use of the dramatic idiom is a self-conscious critical assessment of community and existence. Fuller knows that to live in America is to face death, daily death, if you are a black person. But this death is not necessarily from the hands of a white person although whites have invented the mantras that guide the blacks that despise themselves to commit the same crimes against blackness that whites have committed for centuries. Self-hatred or cultural degradation sits at the door of massive numbers of black-on-black murders. Battling against the overwhelming despair that seems endemic in the black community the dramatist runs as fast as he can, with his words, to resurrect the vitality and energy of a dormant population.

Community can elude us, even as we exist within a community. The critique of community is one way to bring it back to us or rather to return us to our own roots. Language oscillates between the real and the dramatic in a powerful combination of urban reality and stage presentation. But that is not all; Fuller is convinced that the African American community or the gathering of social, cultural, and political artifacts of that community in a linguistic array of words fashioned as drama can display the energy necessary for transformation. In fact, as most writers feel, Fuller knows that words written on paper can impact how people view themselves. Problems can be solved, not simply ignored, by self-conscious engagement with whatever the crisis happens to be. This is the driving spirit of *Zooman*.

I understand Fuller when I see *Zooman* because he is the same deeply emotional man that I am when I see the chaos within the black community. There is something in his work that resonates with the thousands of black writers and thinkers who have been accustomed to seeking resolution of problems. In a way that is the trail of tears for the black writer who is committed to making a difference even while speaking honestly about one's community.

The appearance of our situation in drama is, likewise, the invisibility of the processes by which we found our situation. One does not have enough time on a stage to provide a prosaic account of the multiplicity of ways and means that constitute the processes of our disadvantage, discrimination, segregation, abandonment, and nihilism. We must leave this to the imagination of the dramatist who knows how to appeal to the inexhaustible flow of the ideas in order to carve out a particular space and place in time for us to enjoy and to grieve. Who else but the dramatist can interrupt the flow of a universal discourse and make the invisible visible?

The ancient Africans used to believe that there were only a few approaches to life that mattered and that the search for what mattered included seeking to hear the inaudible, exploring the limits of touch, and seeking to discover how to make that which we do not know materialize as a part of our existence. Indeed, the anarchy of irrational action leading to the death of children is itself a part of the existence of living in a deranged society, even perhaps as deranged people who are made so by the challenge of political, social, and psychological disorientation. Of course, Fuller makes the community the source of responsibility, in fact, a responsibility that it finds at first difficult to accept. Throughout his dramatic career Fuller has sought to discover the sense of responsibility in his characters as an avenue to the souls of the spectators.

In *A Soldier's Play* Fuller has Waters say to Peterson: "There's a trick to it, Peterson—it's the only way you can win—C.J. could never make it—he was a clown!" Of course, for Waters being "like them" meant not being yourself, and Fuller is always himself in the accuracy of his dramatic touch in his plays. He knows precisely the bells to ring and he rings them with deft interaction between characters. The black world exists in the midst of other worlds, with some arbitrariness, but nevertheless with enough certainty of culture to announce some common understandings about the larger white world that we share. I mean Fuller knows in *A Soldier's Play* that Waters should know, and he does know, that the only way "you can win" is to deny your own humanity. Yet this is a heavy price to pay for an impenetrable riddle of a racist society.[1]

In the most fundamental way Fuller is a dramatist in pursuit of truth, not *the truth*, but the relevant and relative truth that can be used to make us better humans. Such betterment in Fuller's terms has to do with making proper judgments about how we live with each other. In effect, this is a fundamentally American ideal in the best sense of that notion. It is not, as one can understand, the racist, bigoted, and white sheet American ideal that came to this country with the ignorance of race supremacy, but rather the more progressive visionary insight that comes with national maturity. We do not have to be like each other; in fact, we do not even have to like each other to be authentic human beings. So long as one's thoughts and dislikes do not bring chaos to the lives of others those dislikes and reflections remain unchallenged by others.

I am struck by the fact that Fuller does not seem to pursue morality in his drama. This is not to say that certain implied ethical behaviors are not present; they are, indeed, they have to be if the playwright is to carry out his own statement of the human condition. But there is no redemption, so to speak, in Fullerian drama because there is no mystic propitiation or expiation. Redemption occurs because someone has broken something, created a fault, and that requires propitiation that leads to redemption. Fuller, despite his training in the Catholic tradition, avoids discovering means of consecration or forcing sacraments on his characters as he re-invents history. If a character is made to express a need for "forgiveness" or "repentance" such a character must find these acts in the natural course of his characterization, but Fuller does not force these sentiments. Fuller's limited emphasis on morality does not mean that he avoids the major issues of human history because drama, and especially Fuller's drama, is a reproduction. I do not mean that he precisely or exactly reproduces history as history but that he makes drama that is also historical.

I really mean that Fuller reproduces history as he makes drama. Taking his philosophical values from a deep well of spirituality that comes from his family and community, Fuller translates the reality of our lives into encounters with history. He elaborates with an aesthetic deftness on the necessity for us to confront both the reality of our contemporary lives and the meaning of our lives within the context of a historical frame.[2]

But the truth is that most history presents itself as indecisive, stark, unrepentant, and unlearning and Fuller must grapple with the incapacity of community, his ideal community, in order to right the role of history. What if the bleakness we see in history when we place our confidence in a failed person or a community is truly permanent? But of course, we know that there are lights, many lights at once sometimes, where a band of brothers and sisters appear capable of shaping their own destinies. This we call progress or an advance on the nature of society. This is what happens when in Fuller's Philadelphia the street gangs came together after much coaxing and prompting on the part of elders to settle differences and to live as if they were in the same house, but this is not the natural state of affairs in a society where the scarcity of goods, inadequate social and psychological services, and scarce money are rampant, almost natural. In such a state we find Zooman where the person believes that he is autonomous, distant, distinct, and unconnected in a way that causes him to bring disorder, chaos, and death. Fuller creates these scenes, shows them to us, and requires of his readers and audiences the ability to ponder what would they do. Our anguish is prolonged and aggravated by our grieving mothers and fathers in the midst of one more shooting and one more death in the community yesterday. The clarity to see the contradictions of place and time and the lucidity to describe those contradictions in words give us the courage to diminish the impact of the chaos. This is where Fuller's *Zooman and the Sign* is most appropriate in its design on human weakness to act.

I recall that during the late summer of 2012 when the numbers of murders in Chicago were on track to reach more than 500 by the end of the year several groups of black preachers, civic leaders, and the Mayor of Chicago, Rahm Emmanuel tried to assess the situation. It seemed that Chicago was imploding with shooting deaths in all parts of the city. There were no more excuses to be given by priests, imams, and preachers about the ineffectiveness of their messages. The youth in the streets empowered with the handgun carried more gravitas than those cloaked in the cloth of piety. They were individually and collectively the Zoomen of the city. While Chicago's crisis is a current situation what Fuller dealt with in *Zooman and the Sign* was something that was predictable in other urban enclaves. Confronted with an underperforming economy, a bleak employment scene, and a lack of historical consciousness, the youth in the cities were drawn and are drawn to many of the social distractions that lead to gun battles, gunshots, and gun wildness in the streets. This situation presented itself to Charles Fuller as a writer as a part of the authentic life experiences of millions of people who live in large cities. We all know what he is writing about when we see the play. But we must be careful not to assume that this was a new reality, it was simply a reality that was picked up by the keen insight of Fuller as a dramatist. He was able to wedge himself, his mind, his intellectual prowess, into the crevices that opened with the pervasive condition of nihilism and violence. A dramatist is not an ideologue but the work of the dramatist is often filled with traces of ideology and Fuller's *Zooman and the Sign* is a protest against the aggressive advance of a vile hooliganism that leads to the death of safety. Fuller knows that the masses of people in the cities seek peace; they do not want to be alienated from their own communities, their own streets, and blocks.

Therefore, we are faced with contemporary and historical realities in a stark existential manner. The retrieval of our sanity often lost in the thickets of ambiguity that come with racial oppression, is a necessity for our collective sense of purpose. How do we know who we are when media, universities, schools, and religious leaders constantly assault us, telling us that they know our identity better than we know ourselves? "Come to rescue" we seem to demand of an intellectual, a dramatist, a thinker, and an artist like Charles Fuller. It is as if we would have had to create a Fuller if he did not exist because the times, 1970s to the 21st century, required someone who could understand our historical situation, mediate our existential condition, and draw the forms and shapes of our identity in the specific terms of new aesthetic drama. The dramatist of history is in constant contact with events, personalities, and situations as avenues to human truths. This allows the dramatist as rescuer to elevate conversation, reveal vulgarities, and excite the possibilities of human action. Fuller affirms the right of African Americans to exist with all of the illusions about history and the present confronted by all of us. How can the African live in the same time and place as others and yet exist in utter disregard of the role of the individual responsible to the collective? Thus, the real problem for Fuller, if there is a problem, is how to advance understanding and entertainment in the context of human responsibility. We are all situated in our human corner seeking to make sense out of the American condition. Fuller knows this and like Malcolm X favors history as the educational link between the past and the future.

The historically rural and the more modern urban environment came to play roles in Fuller's dramatic genre yet Fuller seems comfortable with both the rural and the urban context or perhaps the southern and the northern experiences as sources of dramatic content. He knows, for example, that Africans participated in the Civil War and that the Reconstruction was only thirteen years. There are no blank spaces in his appreciation of the dramatic art form because there are no fatal gaps in his knowledge of history. With Fuller we learn how to transcend the flaws brought by racial animus and a history of discrimination. We see human beings in their individual and collective righteousness. This is critical for the dramatist who writes about black people. Any dramatist who dares to speak or write from a historical fountain of knowledge must understand something about the nature of black nobility. It was, after all, the fact that blacks were in the southern legislatures that led to the public schools, voting rights, jury participation, and Home Rule in the South. Blacks were responsible for outlawing the universally used whipping-posts, the branding irons on human flesh, and the use of stocks for punishment. Furthermore, the generosity of African American democratic ideas meant that the legal system in the South was changed forever. It meant that they were able to reduce the number of legal felonies from 20 to 3; this was an action that benefitted blacks and poor whites that were often the victims of felonies by virtue of certain crimes being considered felonies by race and class. Stealing a chicken was a felony alongside assaulting a man with a knife reminiscent of the marijuana convictions of the late 20th century. Black legislators in their drive to correct injustices that had been perpetrated for generations against their own people undertook the task of making life better for all people. Whatever deserves to be remembered as a part of the African American legacy, Fuller remembers, and even if he does not use all he knows, what he uses impacts his understanding of the historical context. Having demonstrated a full-grown sense of self-consciousness, Fuller is able to concentrate on how blacks in the United States have emerged from a state of resistance to one of advancing a more liberal and human agenda. His appeal is across the generations though his works usually concentrate on the youth.

I do not claim that Fuller's emphasis on youth in the historical context is something that is out of tune with the overall symphony of his work. He understands the dynamic of generation and the tension between generation and tradition. Youth is the preferred age of the generations. Sometimes we say that this or that generation prefers youth but our age is no different. We celebrate youth more than age and this was perhaps true throughout the history of the West, at least, as long as Africans have been in the Western world. Of course, we can say that in Africa and in Asia, maybe in some quaint parts of Europe, untouched by the great wars, there are still values represented by age. The truth is that with age comes knowledge and wisdom that could help us make new discoveries of community and self but then we are too sick and feeble to bring them into being; then comes youth again to the rescue, only to repeat the pattern. What I do claim, however, is that Fuller brings us together with our inadequacies and our possibilities and perhaps more than he realizes, his readers know that he is on a path that ends ultimately in a recurring Sisyphus push of a boulder up the hill one more time. Age has little to do with the hopelessness found in such a routine. We are inescapably led to the same routine.

I hasten to say that age alone is not a panacea for anything, certainly not a solution to the crisis of culture. Fuller also knows this and in each of his major works he underscores the collective sense of wisdom. It is not something that resides in the oldest man or the oldest woman because history has taught us that sometimes the elders are far from appreciating the truth. This is not necessarily the case but it becomes the most frequent response to issues when we are confronted by the conundrums of existence in a world where ethics are often rhetoricized but not often practiced. We become, all over again, in our attempt to return to the source of our communal wisdom, men and women, running away from what are right in front of our eyes. In fact, it may very well be our reflections in the mirror. This is the feeling I get when I see *Zooman* or *A Soldier's Play*. All I have been taught about Hegel or Shakespeare, or Twain or Hemingway, or even the works that I have read of Ellison and Morrison, send me back to myself and I see that I am standing alone before reality. I must decide if the society is responsible for my lack of action in the face of evil or am I willing, passionately willing, to ignore everything that indicates my culpability as a spectator or reader or human being only to point my fingers at someone else.

Fuller's drama extracts from the reader or spectator even the hidden elements of human vulnerability that resides alongside the flexed muscles of what we think we know about ourselves. When I see a play or read a novel I am bringing to the experience everything that I know and everything that I have felt. By observing and entering into *Zooman and the Sign* I sign onto urban living, idealism, fear, enlightenment, reciprocity, imbalance, revenge, and the ultimate reality of death. What we thought we had when we did not realize the extent of the callousness and vile in our neighborhoods is gone. The play once again reminds us of our weakness. There is no protection, no law, no community, and no God. We are left alone like beggars in the street.

In Fuller, the apolitical becomes the political; in fact, the understatement is itself the statement. The dramatist is compelled to sponsor huge billboards along major roads in Philadelphia appealing to youth to renounce violence against each other. After receiving the Pulitzer Prize Fuller joined with his sons and sponsored the anti-violence campaign with huge billboards that dotted his native North Philly. The reality for many Philadelphians was that we saw in powerful terms Fuller's passionate desire for people to love themselves. One asks whether or not this is historical? The answer is that it is as much a part of the historical record as any political act. There is no temporal ambivalence in Fuller's action in creating and exhibiting the billboard; he is responding to a confusion that leads to the murder of hundreds of black people each year. There is a transparency in the billboards that brings out the poverty of our thinking about solutions to absolute violent terror in the neighborhoods. We like to make a distinction between senseless violence and some other form. In the end, any physical violence against another person stems from a senseless place. Therefore, whatever the citizen Fuller does to ameliorate the conditions of violence in his neighborhood must be seen in the light of the playwright Fuller who uses drama to transmute the historical into a present now.

The campaigns for black history and black studies during the 1960s were intended to provoke transformations in the society and changes within the African American people themselves. We were to become the people we had forgotten; history was to make us better because we knew something about the past. What Fuller's art tells us is that history is not the mere repeating of an event or the simple succession of one thing or the other, but rather the living and breathing reality of conflicts within and without us. There are differences in events, personalities, locations, and actions and one cannot reduce one person to another or one event with another. Philadelphia may have similarities with New York but these are different cities and the people are different people; only the dramatist can make us see the collective consciousness that gives us a universal response to our historical condition. We are all in history together; there cannot be a condition of someone else being "in history" and we not being in history. As someone who has studied history for a long time I am convinced that the differences between humans in handling history is our consciousness of it. I know something about the emergence of the black community in South Philadelphia; I have read Du Bois' *The Philadelphia Negro*; I learned about the Underground Railroad from reading William Still's classic; I entered the archives at the Library Company and the Blockson Afro-American Collection and peered deep into the ramping up of neighborhoods and ethnic communities; and I read about the nihilistic moments in the late 20th century when it seemed that the entire city was embroiled in the worst gang violence in the nation. Therefore, I am ready for *Zooman*. I am not claiming that you cannot understand the large implications of *Zooman* without my experiences or similar experiences of someone from a large urban community. There are marks, chords that reflect the general sentiment and tone set by the dramatist that everyone will get, but the person who has some consciousness of the situation will have a different response to the play.

Ultimately, this is the meaning of the reproduction of history. The African American audience is on the first line of this conflict with history as reproduction. We cannot slough the matter from our minds because it consumes our communities. Our aim has always been to transcend the conditions of our situation or the situation of our condition. Inheritors, on one side, of the ancient empires of Africa and, on the other side, victims of the Arab and European Slave Trades, we live between the brutality of that memory and the insanity of our present status in the world, lost in a cul-de-sac, as it were, with only ourselves to depend on for clarity and sanity. Into this trap walk the poet, the scholar, and the dramatist with small lights pointing in the direction of a greater light. This is the true reproduction of history in the dramatic genre and Fuller allows us to see ourselves for who we are.

CHAPTER FOUR

The Shape of Social Truth

Whether form follows matter or matter follows form is a common conundrum that has neither been proved nor disproved by scores of thinkers regardless to their opinion on the issue. What I can say, however, is that the dramatist can, in a measured way, much like an artist molding clay, teach us about the contours of our times. Thus, for Charles Fuller truth is neither ethnic nor racial; it has come to be understood as existing without regard to origin or culture.[1] However, clearly one knows certain facts and establishes certain behaviors and customs on the basis of experiences cultural or otherwise and one is likely to see the shape of social truth through the eyes of one's immediate and historical experiences. Truth, like the Foucaultian sense of power, depends on rules and not on personalities and social institutions. Indeed, personalities and social institutions may embrace the untruth and express their own facts as valid only to be proven wrong and sinister. Charles Fuller understands the shape of social truth but his understanding is different from some of the works of his contemporaries. While one may call his work naturalistic because of the closeness of its shape to real human beings, it is not naturalistic in the stark manner that we see the works of Amiri Baraka and Ed Bullins, two of the most authentic interpreters of African American situations. Fuller is certainly theatrical but theatrical in a way that shows his commitment to an idea of solidarity with truth and that is one of his great calling cards in modern theatre. His characters grow from ignorance to knowledge, from inaction to action, and from childhood thoughts to maturity. In *A Soldier's Play* we are confronted first of all by the amusing dramatic situation of black men together, one of the rarest of theatrical presentations in modern American drama. Fuller knows that his presentation of a variety of black men on a military base is itself a profound statement with many possible readings. This realization itself is only meaningful in the context of the inter-textuality of the play with the larger context of a racist society that finds threats in the idea of black men being together without being in prison or on a plantation guarded by armed whites. Fuller knows that anger, rational anger, is possible in any racial context and that the unfolding of *A*

Soldier's Play reveals all of the avenues for anger. However, Fuller is a deft dramatic writer, a skilled scientist with the gift for precision in description and execution. This is why he is able to say, "My argument is on the stage. I don't have to be angry, O.K.? I get it all out right up there. There's no reason to carry this down from the stage and into the seats. And it does not mean that I am not enraged at injustice or prejudice or bigotry. It simply means that I cannot be enraged all the time. To spend one's life being angry, and in the process doing nothing to change it, is to me ridiculous. I could be mad all day long, but if I'm not doing a damn thing, what difference does it make?"[2] (Fuller, interview, 1982). Even with a play as potentially explosive at every turn as *A Soldier's Play* Fuller is controlled using every aspect of his genius to reveal the capacity of humans, all humans, to break under the weight of a distorted oppressive system.

Humanity precedes culture in Fuller's construction although he does not eliminate cultural considerations from his writing. Situating a group of black men on a military camp and allowing them to come to terms with their own humanity is one way to see how humans are shaped by social setting, cultural upbringing, and the vagaries of experiences that will help define their being. There is almost a Sartrean element in *A Soldier's Play* in the sense that the characters reveal themselves bit by bit until the spectator finally sees the full measure of their humanity. The definitive act of murder and the search for the murderer gives substance to the characterization and makes the shape of social truth dependent upon the dynamic interplay of culture, beliefs, emotions, and attitudes.

In many ways I see Charles Fuller as representing the three fundamental functions of a dramatist. He is self-consciously engaged in the process of creating a new and flexible world where all humans can see themselves reflected as agents and actors in their own capacity and with the will to live in freedom. Thus, he enlarges his own dramatic capability with intellectual and aesthetic notions that allow him to recreate society in his own image. But here again this is not precisely as he would say it, but as I see his characters unfold in the dramas that I have viewed and read he is truly capable of developing a worldview for his characters. Now the fact of the matter is that Fuller is probably more willing to admit to a recreation of society but not to the recreation in his own image that he would see as much too controlling. He rejects the conformity of society and also the strident adherence to any political or ideological system. This is important because while we generally associate dramas with catharsis in local communities in the Western world, this is not necessarily so throughout the world. I am not saying that Fuller rests his case on the African beginnings of drama in the Nile Valley or the Greek inheritance of the West, but is definitely confident that drama must now be opened up to assume a larger role in society.

Secondly, Fuller understands that the dramatist must focus on universalizing the human struggle beyond race and local communities creating a world community that abhors violence, oppression, racism, obscene caricatures of humanity, and violations of persons. He pursues such a world as a free man but not a man unconnected from his origins. He is not detached from the African community in Philadelphia, Toronto, New York, Los Angeles, the Caribbean or the continent of Africa. This attachment is basically his strength as a writer and it is an enduring intellectual appeal to other writers. Lynn Nottage has spoken bravely and brilliantly about her indebtedness to Charles Fuller. As a Pulitzer Prize-winner herself, Nottage understands the fundamental relationship of the writer to the subject. When Oprah Winfrey commissioned an adaption of her Pulitzer Prize-winning play, *Ruined* for television. While the play has some strong sexual elements the fact that it is situated in the Congo during the time of war and terror reminds one of Charles Fuller's penchant for discovering the proper context for human decision-making. Nottage demonstrates the same power of wit and knowledge in *Intimate Apparel* and *Meet Vera Stark*. In some senses Katori Hall's *Hurt Village* might be said to be in the same Fullerian vein. I am not mentioning these authors as direct descendants of Fuller but rather to show that they are related in the way they choose settings, language, and their ability to raise the bar on our expectations. Surely Katori Hall's *Mountaintop* stands as an important piece in the literary tradition of the bravest playwrights who choose topics, interests, themes, and actions that both entertain and teach without being didactic.

Thirdly, he is a dramatist who assumes citizenship in the world and who demonstrates good citizenship by breaking the lines that have been laid in the sand, quietly, like a stealth engine, using all of his natural and cultural traits, to transform the human landscape for the protection of freedom. A Fullerian openness to the world opens him up to questions about his own depiction of black characters. What are the constraints on a dramatist who seeks to right the world, break the back of violence, and humanize the African person as a human with all the frailties of other humans? How does Fuller's use of situations, families, military camps, and other gatherings of giants and not so many giants become a part of the aggregation of facts about his role as a writer?

Are we seeing in Charles Fuller the first evidences of a military discipline, an impression of power, and a generalized desire for order? What is the obsession, if it is an obsession, with law, history and martial arts? Did his experiences as a soldier spill over to his conscious writing of drama? I can see that the stories to be told are too numerous to tell when you are confronted by all the elements of life in the barracks. But I do not believe this is a quest for order for the sake of order, that would be much too sterile in the thinking of Fuller, but rather the confrontation with the reality of death in the city, bizarre nihilism, and wanton terror, causes the dramatist to write about new possibilities. I mean he is begging us to see the facts right in front of our eyes and he is telling us that we are all complicit in the disorder and chaos around us. But the blindness that is produced by too much death and too much terror makes us callous in the face of numerous attempts to gain our participation in salvaging the disintegration of society. As spectators we are confronted by our imagination when the playwright gives us the edited reality of his own imagination and therein is the power of our freedom. We are able by virtue of our own experiences, sometimes limited, to recompose the disintegration of any situation. The ensemble of literary and dramatic tidbits organized to challenge our imagination helps us to construct a meaningful purpose for the play. If Fuller were not able to provide for us these literary responses to chaos, including the chaos inside of us, indeed, inside our communities, we would be impotent to define or defend ourselves. This is why *Zooman and the Sign* is an elegant entry into our confused and chaotic world because it focuses on what we should know about ourselves, and what we should do for ourselves.

How can a random act of urban violence throw a whole community into disarray? One wonders why the people so garrulous have become so silent, so happy have become sad? It is the exploration of this idea that brings *Zooman and the Sign* to the forefront of a dialogue on power and domination. The community is just as terrified of its silence as it is of the crazed teenager. In the silence of fear one recognizes vulnerability and when a community is paralyzed by the threat of violence or, as in this case, the actual committing of a violent act it rips apart all of the social threads that hold us together.

Zooman and the Sign is an explosion of conditions that one could find in any community. Zooman is a youth who has lost his way and he engages in vile acts against members of his own community, mugging, fighting, and sowing pain and grief everywhere he goes, an indication that he is on the prowl for the weakest people in the society. Yet when Jinny Tate, the 12-year old daughter of hardworking parents, trying to resolve their marital problems, is accidentally shot in a neighborhood overrun by hatred, disregard, and violence, the play finds its generative power. Rachel and Emmett Tate find it within their hearts to come together around their grief and perhaps to save their marriage. Rachel wants to be left alone to mourn her loss but her husband wants to find the killer. Just as much as Rachel is hurt to the core by the loss of her child, her husband is condemned by his hatred for the killer of his daughter. Their son, Victor, succeeds in getting a gun from a friend of his in order to go out and look for the killer. The discovery of Victor's gun causes additional pain and distress as the family seeks to work out a way to resolve their grief, pain, and desire for both vengeance and justice. Seeking assistance from his neighbors to find the killer, Tate is overwhelmed by the disregard with which his neighbors confront his situation. They are relatively unmoved by grief and pain. They distrust the police and they are unwilling to speak out about the crime fearing that they could be the next victims. Some of them saw the crime committed, they were on their front porches when the shooting occurred but they did not see anything. In rage and distraught, Emmett hangs a sign that reads "THE KILLERS OF OUR DAUGHTER JINNY ARE FREE ON THE STREETS BECAUSE OUR NEIGHBORS WILL NOT IDENTIFY THEM." Of course, this does not bring the neighbors to the side of the Tate family; they are enraged that he would bring attention to his neighbors in this way. For the most part the neighbors try to avoid the Tates. A few friends arrive, Donald Jackson, who brings food, and Grace Georges, whose daughter had been Jinny's friend, try to convince Emmett to take down the sign. Ultimately Emmett believes that they are self-serving rather than concerned about the pain and grief of the Tate family. The neighbors believe that their lack of action to help with solving the crime should not be made public by the sign because Emmett's sign is telling the world that the neighborhood is unsafe and made up of cowards.

There are implications in both of these stated signals. If the neighborhood is unsafe then there is a financial implication having to do with the price of property and the perception of a neighborhood being unsafe triggers all types of responses. In fact, more Zoomen may enter the community and make it a haven for criminals. Secondly, the fact that the neighbors may be cowards is personal and collective; people see themselves as persons with dignity and courage and to call them cowards hits them in the central nervous system of their own self-concept.

Other family members, Emmett's uncle Reuben and Rachel's

cousin, come to their assistance. Fuller has these older family members, sort of a wise chorus, make strong observations about the transformations in the black community over time. Families and communities were closer, people knew how to protect and assist each other, and children were more obedience, and so forth. Ash goes so far as to say that food stamps are destroying the fabric of the community because people just eat junk food and stay home and watch television. She says, "When the Negroes were hungry we treated each other better." There is no solution to the violence in the community; there is only resolution to the crisis in the neighborhood. Ash could have said something even more about our previous state of existence and that is that we had less access to handguns. This may have taken the play out of bounds, however. Of course, Fuller does not want to preach and has no business in the preaching business anyway and therefore he leaves the problem squarely where his imagination found it in the community, actually in a very small corner of the larger black community. Emerging from a solid African American family himself and having married two, not simultaneously, intelligent black women, Miriam and Claire, and raising two strong black sons, Charles III and David Ira, Fuller could have preached, he could have insisted on a didactic method for his plays, but all of the artist in him moved him away from such an easy course. He took the road of symbolism, aesthetics, icons, suggestive and alternative realities, and phased characters who could pass through one stage and onto the next without the spectator really understanding what had happened until the play was nearly over. This is why he could be seen as the best dramatist of his era. Ralph Ellison produced one great novel and a couple of books of essays and memoirs and we still recognize the power of what he did in *Invisible Man*, whether we agree politically or not. The book is a monument much like *A Soldier's Play* is on its way to becoming, not so much because it won for Fuller the Pulitzer Prize but because it established a powerful truth about family, community, and nation.

In reality, Charles Fuller's *Zooman and the Sign* centers on the chaos brought into a family by the death of a little girl, but she could have been anyone, a man, woman, old or young. Fuller gives us one of the most vulnerable and therefore most innocent victims possible. The death of the child sets in motion actions that are represented in every community where disorder, degradation, fear, lack of education, and violence converge to challenge life and to make death too common. The spectator is offered an imagination brimming with fears and contradictions, possibilities and certainties, and the inevitability that we will have to confront family, community, and humanity. *Zooman and the Sign* serves up Jinny Tate, an innocent like the endless bands of innocents one finds in New York, London, Paris, Chicago, Shanghai, Rio de Janeiro, or Johannesburg, or the town next to ours. What Fuller is intent on doing is showing us that this is not just a tale about urban life, though it is situated in a city, and cities bring with them their own assumptions and difficulties, but for this most urbane of dramatists, *Zooman and the Sign* is not just a narrative about urban life; it is preeminently a metaphor, indeed, a trope full of every conceivable chaos, rage, anger, condemnation, and hellfire that could be imagined in the a monster's head. Over there is recrimination, down the street is deceit, and right here in our own space is disbelief and lies!

Thus, Fuller's innocent Jinny Tate forms a plinth from which the playwright raises a whole host of issues. The senseless, arbitrary, and accidental death of Jinny is like a nadir of grief, hopelessness, and pain. Where the audience would see disappointment and feel the incredible urge to make sense out of the senselessness one finds the light of clarity as Fuller allows the characters to work from this low point to a resolution on the stage. I have found few dramatists who know how to write from the abyss as Fuller does. He is at once brilliant in producing contradictions and equally skilled in saving us from our worst fates. Clearly he is sometimes misunderstood as Amiri Baraka misunderstood *The Soldier's Play* when in 1983 he wrote in the *Black American Literature Forum* that "I always try to hook up Fuller to Russell's Five on the Black Hand Side, which was a pretty superficial look at the contradictions in the black community, particularly between the "integrationist" sector and the cultural nationalists. .... The captain tracks the militant down, condemning him because he lacks compassion for the black-hating sergeant. **Fuller** says that is our real problem, that the black militants lack compassion for the black-hating Negroes."³ I will return to *A Soldier's Play* later but one sees a prominent, creative dramatist such as Baraka, basically drawing attention to what he sees as a problem in Fuller's drama. On the other hand, the Turkish writer, Nilgun Anadolu-Okur, writing from an Afrocentric theoretical position in her book *Contemporary African American Theater: Afrocentricity in the Works of Larry Neal, Amiri Baraka, and Charles Fuller,* describes Fuller as maintaining a "more flexible repertory" of works from a social realism base.⁴ But Fuller's drama is not problematic to any one who knows African American experiences; it is ethical, forthright, and demanding. Fuller does not ask Foucault's ethical question, "What can I become?" Instead, he seeks to discover if Africans can transcend the condition that has made them truly human in the worst ways. His question is, "What ought we to become?"

Fuller's "ought" is full of promise because as an optimist the playwright is plowing his way through a multiplicity of human possibilities. We become daily and we are prone to engage in various attitudes and actions that show us how we are becoming but the real deal is what ought we to become given our situations. We are situated in the midst of nihilistic tendencies, aggressive warfare against and among black people, and a sustainable poverty that devastates our will. Racism, the grand master, manipulates all of these situations.

As a dramatist with a historian's insight Fuller draws the ethical and historical dimensions of African American life into one single thread of communal relationship with no regard to one's station, occupation, or situation. While I am deeply influenced in my reading of his texts by my own prioritizing of history I am nevertheless content that my reaction to Fuller's dramatic burden is in keeping with the most objective analysis one can make. In my reading I wanted to ask Fuller, "What service could you make to the advancement of the African American community by breaching the myths of infallibility that had filled too many plays?" Yet it was clear, sooner rather than later, as I undertook my reading of his texts that he was always moving toward a rhythm of transformation. There is no negativity in his ambition for the African American community. By iteration and citation of historical incidents, phrases, and places in his dramatic texts Fuller raises the bar for other dramatists to tackle art as useful for living. When Lydia Diamond gives us *Stick Fly* as an iteration of race and class from the perspective of wealthy blacks she is in effect, dramatizing in the same way as Fuller. The handling of the issues of race is different but the elements of our history in the United States are unavoidable. This is why I am not saying that Fuller is the only one who does this but rather that Fuller has given us a pattern in his drama that highlights the acceptance of history and race as companions to good drama.

Yet there is something else that must be said about Fuller the dramatist. He is a historical being himself as well as being in history and a maker of history with his drama. To decipher this statement one only has to understand that the inaccessibility to the estate of history for most people is real even in its most demeaning aspects. However, to be a historical being one must realize through consciousness that he or she is living in a memorable moment in time. Fuller's entrance into the literary arena during the period of great racial turmoil meant that with consciousness he was himself a historical being. However, he was also a being in history alongside the masses of us who were living our lives in ordinary times. Yet as a dramatist Fuller is able to access history as a creator of characters, plots, actions, and themes that make history. Such ability as a writer takes numerous skills of structure and memory.

Iconic nostalgia as an association of ideas, facts, expressions and energies is one of Fuller's greatest achievements as a dramatist. It is as if the dramatist insists that the spectator or reader must learn something in the process of being impacted by the dramatic adventure. When one strips away the debris of life iconic nostalgia remains constant and anchoring. Fuller knows African American history very well from reading Du Bois, Benjamin Quarles, Lerone Bennett, and Carter G. Woodson while serving as the keeper of library books when he was in the army. Thus, he is aware that for 250 years African people in the United States were outside of the dramatic discourse although there were some black writers and actors who contributed to the theater during this time. Yet Fuller also knows, as his plays show, that one must always pack the lines with enough nostalgia that the audience is able to stake their emotions on the historical foundation of the drama. His associations are always governed by a humanist's desire to share with others the historical icons of the black community. But more, Fuller is a teacher, a professor, who believes that the black community must be reintroduced to itself. He is enamored by the nobility of his people, their courage, sense of myth, iconic fragments held onto from the African past, and their ability to survive in the midst of chaos. The author translates this knowledge into bundles of authentic dramatic historical sparks. Thus, in *A Soldier's Play* Fuller knows that history is on top of history, that is, the play represents a historical frame and the iconic nostalgia within the text ties the knowledgeable audience to an array of narratives pieces of history. This layering of history on top of other histories often conceals the genuine feelings of nihilism, anarchy, fatalism, optimism, victorious consciousness, and joy that's a part of the human condition.

As we pivot to a look at *Zooman and the Sign* again we have to raise another point: the contemporary demand of history. This play is set in the present and has the authenticity of urban life in the same sense that *A Soldier's Play* had military authenticity. Fuller was a child of the 1960s when two wars were going on in the black community. One war was within the community and it was called gang war and the other was between the black community and the white colonial occupier of inner cities.

Gang violence in Fuller's Philadelphia seemed almost endemic because of the intense neighborhood character of the row house streets. One could find some streets where families lived for several generations in the same houses. Everyone knew the neighbors and no one tolerated strangers. Rules existed on the streets. Everyone knew what was expected and what was not tolerated. If a stranger wandered into some neighborhoods they would be immediately questioned or accosted. In fact, xenophobia existed in the 1960s that devastated communities with suspicion and violence. I think what Fuller showed by dramatizing this situation was that the old myth of non-violence in the black community was simply more complicated than we had believed. It was not true that black people did not fight and did not kill; it was more that the killing was often done within our own communities. We killed each other. This was an uncomfortable fact since some people had thought that black people were non-violent almost by nature! Of course, this was not true, as Fuller understood, black people were just as violent as other humans. America had not evolved a new type of person, a non-violent African. I think this is why John Oliver Killens would say that such a nonviolent individual bore no relationship to any primate he knew. Zooman was in fact a universal character.[5]

Lester Johnson, the rough character in *Zooman and the Sign*, who gives monologues about his life and the nature of violence, is someone found in many urban areas. In this play Rachel Tate orders her young daughter Jinny, who is acting out because of the estrangement of her parents, out of the house and she goes out and sits on the steps just as Lester catches a glimpse of someone he has been looking for in the crowded street. He starts shooting and accidentally kills Jinny. Reuben Tate comes to the house to grieve. He is Rachel's estranged husband. The police canvassed the neighborhood in search for witnesses to the shooting. They could find no one to come forward although Victor, Jinny's older brother, has heard in the streets that the shooter is Lester Johnson, known as Zooman.

In a monologue Zooman is unrepentant about the killing and says, "How'm I suppose to feel guilty about that?" He blames the death of Jinny on her being in the wrong place at the wrong time. He takes no blame for the situation and shows no remorse because to him the death of Jinny is just a part of life and death in the community.

Reuben, on the other hand, is greatly agitated by the loss of his daughter. He is angry that none of the neighbors seem to have courage enough to come forward and point the finger at Zooman. Frustrated he puts up his sign saying that the killers are on the streets because the neighbors will not identify them. This angered some of the neighbors because they did not like the fact that television crews came to the neighborhood.

After Jinny's memorial service a brick was thrown threw the window of the Tate's home. Rachel begs Reuben to take the sign down. He refuses but later that night Zooman begins to attack the sign with his knife. He is confronted and shot dead by Emmett, Reuben's brother, as the family comes out of the house.

Fuller's characters are in enmeshed in the thickets of social devastation. Zooman is raised without a father and in one of his monologues speaks to the fact that he had not seen his father much in his life. He takes no blame for any of his negative actions and has no conscience about the killing. He may be the perfect thug, callous and cold, with no regard for life.

Furthermore, the directors and producers who bring *Zooman and the Sign* to stage do so because they recognize the power of the play to provoke change in social situations. It is not an easy play because we are disturbed by its force, by its clarity about who we are in our own homes, and this disturbance is not merely physical but psychological, social, and profoundly ethical. Fuller has found his talent in selecting themes and ideas that project his universal understanding of conditions and situations although the local instances are African American cultural scenes. This is as it should be in the best writers who are always trying to master the human condition from the place they are at the moment. They are deeply attuned to what's around them, the scenes are not merely chosen; the scenes are presented, given as it were, by the very nature of living in the midst of circumstances. In *Zooman and the Sign* we are confronted with youth violence something that is characteristic of many societies; this is not just an African American problem found in Philadelphia, Los Angeles, and New York. Youth and gang violence is a universal phenomenon where young people are disconnected from the values of their societies. We find it in Ireland and Israel, in South Africa and Nigeria, in France and in Albania. Yet what Fuller understands, and the producers who produce his plays accept, is that while his play, *Zooman and the Sign*, is set in an African American community the condition it exposes and the problems it confronts are universal. Now, of course, neither Charles Fuller nor the producers are naïve enough to believe that these problems are in every community or are as intense as they are in some communities. These are problems that come with the breakdown of traditions, the smashing of legitimate codes of conduct, and the erasure of values and virtues. Youth violence and gang chaos often produce bizarre eruptions of human emotions and therefore, finding a way out of the entanglements of our moral encounters is a real search for sanity. Lou Bellamy, the artistic director at Penumbra in Minneapolis, said, "I read a number of recently written plays on this subject and I still think *Zooman and The Sign* is the best. Charles Fuller is careful to show Zooman as scary but also as human and this is what sets this play apart from others. Fuller takes the time to show that Zooman is afraid and wounded and that is what makes him even scarier, like Bigger Thomas in *Native Son*."[6] By placing Fuller's character in the same realm as Richard Wright's Bigger Thomas, Lou Bellamy is suggesting a depth of character that marks the play as profoundly important in examining the root of violence.[7]

To say that the issues are universal, at least, in urban communities where people have been loosed from their traditions is not to minimize the situation of street violence in some of our largest cities in the United States. On the concrete and asphalt streets of Detroit, Philadelphia, New York, Compton, East St. Louis, Camden, and Chicago, too often the insanity of turf wars and power struggles play out in front of our families. While we see it as a current or contemporary situation, it has existed for a long time in the United States. The fact that Fuller, relying on his extensive knowledge of the past, brings it to the forefront in *Zooman and the Sign* is a testament to his ability to build characters that show contradictions of class, religion, race, immigration, and age. One can imagine how stray bullets, those shot in rage against someone or something, can create cauldrons of confusion, hatred, and astonishment. We are stunned by the fragility of life and dumbfounded when stray bullets kill anyone, especially those we see as innocent of any violence, wrong-doing, or hatred, but we must know, and we do know while watching or reading *Zooman and the Sign* that this is the human condition. We will not know everything and we will not be able to explain anything about this situation other than the physical death. The absolute question of "why" is not even possible to answer. Shooters spraying bullets indiscriminately at houses and cars for as long as guns have been around have killed people. Innocent people, bystanders, and passers-by have lost their lives on the stoops stoops of Boston and New York, the row houses of Baltimore, and the neighborhoods of Denver and Minneapolis where children have been struck by bullets meant for someone else. Like a contagion these incidents appear to be without reason and without purpose yet they continue to be relevant to any discourse on solving the violence issue. Nothing can solve the problem of gun-carrying, gangsta-style, low-riding mimics of other thugs who kill innocents while menacing their own communities but the strength and resolve of the community itself.

Tupac Shakur and Notorious B.I.G. may have been the epitome of street credibility in terms of toughness, navigators of the streets, steel men, carriers of the male ethos in the hood, but they were both victims of the milieu that they helped to create and maintain. I remember when 50 Cent, another rapper, was said to have been shot nine times, meaning that he had nine lives, and the media celebrated him for survival in the midst of the hellhole of agony in his community. In my book, *Erasing Racism: The Survival of the American Nation*, I spent considerable time discussing the role of the gun in the African American community. The assertion of a male identity as gun-toting and gun-wielding ramrod of death that defies death creates a mock society, fake and false, which mimics the worst aspects of the criminal enterprise. Fuller sees the senselessness of this scenario and as an intellectual is able to offer an artistic instrument for us to examine ourselves. This is the fulfillment of one of the key roles of the dramatist.

Thus, Fuller is both a dramatist and a prophet in the sense that some of what he saw, experienced, and imagined existed and would exist long after *Zooman and the Sign* had been produced many times. Can a play solve a social problem? The aim of *Zooman and the Sign* is not to solve these issues, not to create a utopian world, but to challenge us and indeed we are challenged by this play as we may have been confronted by turmoil in the past. Here it is authentic, virile violence, maybe of a gang member, maybe not, but visible and powerful killing of dreams. It is the nine-year old girl shot down in Tucson, Arizona, in 2010 when Democratic Congresswoman Gabrielle Giffords was shot; the same nonsense that caused the nine year old to be shot and killed by Jared Loughner happens too often in our cities.

What bizarre twisted sickness causes James Holmes to kill twelve people in a theater in Aurora, Colorado? Who fails to connect the gun violence of Newtown, Connecticut, where Adam Lanza, a 20 year old gun enthusiast, killed 26 people in an elementary school to the overall nature of violence woven in the social cloth of America? Gun violence is not black or white or Latino; it is cold, dumb, ignorant, often deranged stupidity of the worst kind that takes innocent lives and throws us into an inferno of shame, pity, disgust, and anger. We know that violence is not monochromatic and that thug-life artists with influence could be as popular and white as Eminem, and electronic games of murder, war, and chaos can create the formats for violent acts. This is why Fuller's target is not simply race, but the conditions created by the inequalities, dysfunctions of class structure, poverty, marginal education, and institutional, that is, structural conditions that support racial abuse of African people or for that matter, any people.

Since Fuller's play scores of crazed gunmen have killed or maimed hundreds of people. Over 60 mass murders have been committed since 1982. We remember only the most dramatic cases. James Eagan Holmes shot 70 people in a movie theater in Aurora, Colorado; Jeffrey Weise massacred students with a Glock handgun in Red Lake, Minnesota; Seung Hui Cho kills 33 and wounds 23 at Virginia Tech; Eric Harris and Dylan Kiebold murders 15 and injures 24 at Columbine High School in Colorado; and Gang Lu shoots six people to death at the University of Iowa, and so forth. Of course, the 2012 Newtown, Connecticut massacre by Adam Lanza left 26 children and adults dead. in the Fuller's sharpness in *Zooman and the Sign* is that he tells the story of relationships; the play is not ideology but a commentary on society only in the sense that the lives of the characters are real and memorable. On the other hand, Zooman is not a mass murderer; he is motivated by different passions and is an outsider to his society who is known and recognized by the neighbors. This is why Zooman's situation is different from that of mass murderers who hide in plain sight among the masses of people. He is seen and known in his waywardness but the community is cowed by its fear and will not confront him. This is the case with many urban killers and Fuller is quite aware of the social fabric that has been ripped in the neighborhood and has his characters seeking to mend it.

What we see in *Zooman and the Sign* is virtue. In a country where virtue is hard to come by ordinarily because we are pursuing the crass, brassy materialism that parades as success, Fuller brings us to virtue in this play. But this virtue is not a whim or some chimera rather it is found in an act of courage, actually acts of courage, as people, come on board to defend their values. If one can find a virtuous man or woman, one can find courage to protect, defend, and fight for harmony and balance in society; this struggle cannot be engaged by people without virtue. Even if those without virtue are in the play they are superficial, better yet, superfluous to the reality of virtue. When do we know that virtue exist if not when we must show ourselves to be courageous; this is the real meaning of virtue.

Charles Fuller seeks a work where men and women recognize the need to expend themselves in acts of virtue. Despite our social conditions and our surroundings that speak of destruction, destitution, and anxiety, we are not devoid of the possibility of virtue. These are not selfish acts but acts in the interest of the society; they are social acts to and for the common good. Who will rally our communities, like the 54th Massachusetts troops did, to storm the Fort Wagners that threaten our society even if to do so means that we confront our own death? Fuller knows that it is inside us, that is, this fire for truth, this zeal for life and it is neither an illusion nor a delusion, but the very matter out of which we define our values.

The United States is not alone in dramatic, traumatic violence, but it stands out as one of the most violent society because of its history of dispossession of the Native Peoples and the enslavement of the African People. It is impossible to dispossess people of their homeland or to enslave a proud people and deprive them of their freedom without brutal forms of violence. Furthermore, the idea of winning the western lands in America brought with it the destruction of the homes of the Native Peoples and the use of the gun as a bringer of death to those who would stand in the way of "advancing civilization," thus violence is almost as common in American history "as apple pie." We are aware of the role of the gunslinger in the West, the cowboy who is the fastest on the draw, and so forth and therefore, while we are still stunned by the Columbine, Oklahoma City, Cold Spring, Red Lake, or Tucson killings, we are not unaccustomed to trauma of the most gruesome type. Like a military unit under fire we may close our eyes, stay indoors, and watch the wrath of youth senselessness on television, but we cannot forget that these youths are a part of our society. They are *us* in a real sense; they are our history, our culture, and our stupidity. We are also appalled, resistant to defeat, determined not simply to wait out the gunfire but to wade into the water and confront the terror in the territory of our minds and physical spaces. Charles Fuller's play *Zooman and the Sign* reminds us of where we have been, indeed, where we still are after urban renewal, gentrification, black removal from the inner cities, black mayors, and higher taxes. How do we tackle the issues brought forth in Fuller's imagination without having to see another child die or another community explode in violence? Are we ready to impose curfews everywhere, even on ourselves, or must we fight for sanity and humanity in a concerted, dedicated manner? *Zooman and the Sign* is a remarkable instructional tool for those who seek to improve the condition of society. Now, this is not to take away the artistic brilliance of this work but to suggest that like all great art this play has the possibility of being used in numerous way to teach others how to avoid the dangers of chaos brought about by violence. I do not know for a fact but I do not believe this was the aim of Fuller in writing this play; he is at once a dramatist, an artist with a powerful sense of human emotions engaged in the resolution of difficult situations. This is the particular niche he has carved out for himself. I find that *Zooman and the Sign* is full of narratives but the overall meaning of the play may be couched in its metaphors. This is the artistic side of the dramatist; this is ultimately what it means to be an artist as well. We are predisposed to view this play as entertainment but while we are captured by the story, entertained by the interactions of the characters we are brought to the point of true reality when we see the importance of the sign to the Tate family.

Fuller calls the shooter, Zooman. Someone one asked, "Could a white writer have called the black gunman, Zooman?" The answer to that question is "it depends." I mean could a black writer call Loughner, Zooman? There is a sense of the bestiality that comes with the senseless use of a gun; this is not a racial or cultural classification. I believe that the author of the play searched for an appropriate metaphor that captured the gunman's betrayal of culture, lack of respect for the elderly, bad manners, disregard for authority, and moral impotence. He was in fact Zooman, a universal Zooman, someone devoid of understanding the human code of conduct and the decency that governs society. Yet one sees that when Zooman encounters Victor there were some possibilities of humanity. Now we can question what we would have done as writers with the ending. Would we have changed the original sign about Jinny with the final sign about Zooman? Here the playwright uses all of his mental skill to leave the audience with a resolution.

CHAPTER FIVE

The Language of Defiance

Language is the micro-mechanism for all social constructions; it is the atomic structure for all drama. In fact, the theatres may be rivers but the tributaries that build those rivers are truly the rules of language. It is at the level of words that a dramatist like Fuller is able to translate all of his knowledge, elliptical emotions, and perspectivist experiences to the theatre. Fuller's words drive us to the point where we are confronted by our own inability to see that we must do something. Here we are stuck, tricked, forced to be cathartic. The dramatist leads us to the precipice; we must act. There is no turning back when you are hemmed in by violence that scares the hell out of you. There is no way that we can leave the space without fighting, without threatening the abuser, without trampling on the danger and regaining our senses and freedom even when we see our own weakness.

Translating our fear into risk-taking is the road to freedom.

Fuller is a master of language who believes that "foul language" is no indication of genius. In fact, he has argued in an interview in 2011 that profane language and curse words demonstrate that the writer is unable to write good literature.[1] He does not argue for a prohibition of curse words but rather he appeals to the writer to advance the reader, to enlighten the audience, and to build language and knowledge capacity. He does not forget to challenge our intellect as he challenges our imagination with his work. A constitutive element of dramatic works is agency and the idea of agency in a theatre of being is at its core the existence of a way of life that engages the African person at every level. But Fuller is not just writing for blacks; he is writing for his spectators around the world. What he finds in his drama about the lives of blacks he sees in the lives of other people as well. This is his victory. The philosopher Lewis Gordon has coined the term Africana Existentialism to capture the essence of African reflection, presence, and action in the contemporary world.[2] Instead the term Africana Existentialism I prefer to call Fuller's total engagement with society a form of theater of agency after the Afrocentrists who argue that the key to transformation is subjective action. During the period of slavery in the United States the plantation was divided into those who worked in the house and those who worked on the outside. The Mistress of the house was in charge of the activities of the house and the Master was in charge of the activities outside. There is no question that Fuller is attuned to the historical record that announces the African American population as descended from these two sectors of the slave economy. In fact, those inside the house were divided into the mammy, the cook, the washerwoman, the seamstress, the maid, the butler, the porter, the gardener, and the coachman. While these nine roles were typical there could be other titles and positions added to the enslaved Africans in the house. On the other hand, the field Africans, those who worked outside the home were also divided by roles. The outsiders could be headmen, carpenters, porters, planters, butchers, ranchers, harvesters, or woodcutters. In writing from the vantage point of history, Fuller is aware of the historical roots of his characters even if he does not bring them forward as other playwrights have done because he is interested in universalizing his characters in such a way that someone in Japan or Austria might read or see these characters as real, concrete, genuine. This is not to say that the Malcolmian *house Negro* and *field Negro* as constructions would not make sense to Fuller, but rather that Charles Fuller, as an intellectual and a dramatist, sees variations and nuances of beings; this is Fuller's strength as a writer. He repeats in his work the overarching idea that Africans are human beings with the same needs, desires and attitudes as millions of other people on the earth. In effect, to be black is to be human regardless of the various historical roles we find ourselves in this era. One should not have to make this argument in connection with drama or any other discipline but the peculiar history of the United States, a history we are just now truly beginning to understand at a national level, requires a strong reinforcement of a common humanity.

Our world abounds with anonymity, nihilism, lethargy, violence, and prejudice because we have been split from our spiritual past. Although Fuller does not pretend to serve as our minister to uplift our spirits, he does provide us with understanding that will empower us to fight through the chaos of contemporary cultural cowardice. What else is a dramatist to do?

When religion vanished and God abandoned the black communities to urban chaos wrung from the remnant prejudices of a white supremacist beginning and the hellish life of enslavement it was necessary for Africans in the United States to turn to self-determination. If, as Fuller understands, we are neither fowl nor beast but men and women, humans, there is nothing else for us to do than to self activate, to stop the gang-banging, the descent into groveling in the mud. We are really on our own.

Since Fuller does not call himself a philosopher and is as much an anti-minister as any postmodern writer he has to be granted a tradition: Langston Hughes, James Baldwin, Zora Neale Hurston, August Wilson, Larry Neal, Ntozake Shange, and Charles Fuller. Some would typically add Ed Bullins and Amiri Baraka but one could easily propose an alternative heritage for Fuller's drama that includes Bullins, Neal, Baraka, Sonia Sanchez, and Haki Madhubuti. However, Fuller has never admitted to any specific tradition except the Black Arts Movement along the Washington-Philadelphia-New York axis that was a part of the youthful artistic response to the Black Power Movement among poets, choreographers, painters, sculptures, and dramatists. Larry Neal, Fuller's artistic and activist colleague, and Charles Fuller were at the center of the movement.

Although Charles Fuller was born in Philadelphia he found his fame two hours up the New Jersey Turnpike in New York City. In the fertile atmosphere of the New York theatre community Fuller found the intellectual and cultural environment that would allow him to explore this new theatre of being. Douglas Turner Ward, playwright and artistic director, a close friend of Charles Fuller, who created the Negro Ensemble Company as a space where theatre could flourish without having to mince words, conform to white expectations, and feel freedom of expression. Black writers had often complained about not having enough good theaters to produce their works. White producers were wary of offending their white audiences and therefore would produce only those black writers who would appease the producers and audiences. Ward's vision was to create the NEC. He threw himself into this venture wholeheartedly and worked 18-hour days to fulfill his dream.

Ward's theatre dreams helped Fuller and a host of black playwrights realize their creative ambitions and this professional combination advanced African American theatre in America. Fuller saw NEC as a marvelous place for staging his works. The NEC team was devoted to art, theatre, and the most professional performances, and Fuller could be as eloquent as he wanted to be knowing full well that there were voices, producers, actors, who would add flavor, put on brakes, and say, right on brother. The playwrights' works were inspired and their art advanced the African American theatre.[3] NEC was the first black theatre group to explore the most excellent forms of the art. It would later have imitators who would also do excellent work like Penumbra and others. While some of these theatres no longer exist due to financial problems and other difficulties, they were inspired by a generation that showed what could be done. Penumbra became extremely important as a theatre producer of Charles Fuller and August Wilson.[4]

Fuller believes that theatre must transform and transport the audience toward a new reality. What is theatre if it is not to mystify, create movement, and advance ethics? Fuller trounces the work of a playwright that does not move, pursue, and generate true drama. For him, life is dramatic, not static, not a mere discussion, not simply a discussion or an essay but the reality of people doing, that is, acting. He has always been acutely aware of the artistic tradition in the American society and knew that there were negative representations of blacks that had to be avoided, indeed, condemned if necessary. No African American growing up in the United States of America during the 1950s and 1960s could escape the negation of blackness everywhere in the society. White racial domination was waning but it had not been defeated in the minds of whites, and in some places, we have yet to see its real decline in the thinking of white people. Fuller knew this and understood that the message of the theater could not simply be comedy; it had to be serious drama for him. Now the idea of comedy is not trivial and I do not intend to argue that Fuller was against comedy since I have never read or heard him inveigh against it. Nevertheless it is clear to those who read his writings that he casts himself as a serious character because of the deep and penetrating problems that he finds in the society. Negative images of blacks were the substance of most white American books and popular culture before the 1960s. Blacks, too, drank from this polluted well.

For example, a black writer could not repeat the Mulatto, Mammy, Jezebel or Sambo images created for racist white pleasure. While white dramatists could paint the faces of actors black and parade on stage like they were black people when everyone in the audience knew they were whites in jest, no self-respecting black artist would waste their talent in such theatre. Of course, Douglas Turner Ward and Charles Fuller were far from producing this type of theatre. They knew, from history, that the African Grove Theatre, which first appeared in 1821 and was created by William Henry Brown and James Hewlett, had been a first attempt by blacks in the United States to form a professional theatre. They also knew the discrimination difficulties that the African Grove had faced in New York. They were students enough of American theatre to know that Ira Aldridge had left the United States for Europe because of racism in the 19th century. They knew that black theatre companies like the African Grove and others were forced to produce Shakespeare and other dramas from Western theater because of the dearth of plays written by blacks at the time. Yet the African Grove Theatre did venture in 1823 to produce Brown's *The Drama of King Shotaway*, the first play written by an African in the United States. Like other black artists in America, Brown was opposed, harassed, and condemned by whites. The racist nature of the American art community could not believe or accept the fact that Africans were intelligent, gifted actors, and clever writers. Although the theatre played to black audiences in Lower Manhattan it had to close its doors because it could not rent or buy a proper space, so virulent was the anti-black attitude among whites. It would be one hundred years later, in 1923, that the first dramatic play written by an African would be produced on Broadway. This work was called *The Chip Woman's Fortune* written by Willis Richardson. During the Harlem Renaissance in the next decade, the great writers Langston Hughes, Zora Neale Hurston, Jean Toomer and other Harlem Renaissance giants would produce a torrent of African American drama and become important intellectuals and dramatists by virtue of their talent and popularity. Finally, to break the spell of Broadway the play "Raisin' in the Sun," by talented Lorraine Hansberry would be produced and performed in 1959 as the first play to be both directed and written by blacks on Broadway. Lloyd Richards was the director and the play opened up American theatre once and for all times. African Americans, however, did not find it easy to gain acceptance by the producers of Broadway. Thus, Douglas Ward Turner's ingenuity in producing black plays Off Broadway created an entirely new and different clientele for New York drama. Charles Fuller, a card-carrying original of the NEC, emerged as its finest dramatist and certainly its most famous when "A Soldier's Story" was produced and acclaimed as a brilliant production. In one sense, Fuller had found his space, a space prepared by Turner, where he could be free to explore all of the ramifications of his people's being in America.

If as Hamlet said, "The play's the thing wherein I'll catch the conscience of the king," then Fuller, as keen as Shakespeare's character, demonstrates that the play is the arena where *we be*. I do not mean this only in the Ebonics sense of our presence, our existence, but also as the stage where we both perform and see performance. In actuality the play is the place where everything happens, for and against us, uplifting us and crushing us, killing us and saving us; it is the convergence of human life lived. The challenge to this authentic space and situation will be the drama of religion on Sunday mornings in the black churches, but alas, that is another story to be told.

I see *A Soldier's Play* as an entry into the convergences of our complex lives in a society that was based on race. The Founding White Fathers did not conceive of a society without the race factor; it was actually a very large part of their unconscious and conscious being. But Africans were not non-being; indeed we were quite essentially in the fabric of the American soul. Thus, when Fuller draws his characters for *A Soldier's Play* he is creating out of the material that exists full-blown in our communities. One sees these characters everyday and one can see them in every place because they are the real *Everyman* in the African's worldview. Already in 1969 in one of his earliest plays, *The Village: A Party*, Fuller had sought to represent the various aspects of the human personality confronted with race, mixed race, and the tensions often found in society. His characters are literally engaged with each other in a tension that is as real today as it was in the late 1960s. *The Village: A Party* could possibly be read in post modern terms as a trope on the idea of race where the drama surrounds the socially constructed idea that race is biological in such a way that the fluidity of the situation is revealed. Who ultimately is black, mixed, or white? What does it mean anyway given the existential situations that occur regardless to our DNA?

Here is the situation. Between the nationalism of African American militants of the 1960s and the rash integrationists that characterized some members of the George Schuyler (*Pittsburgh Courier* conservative writer) school of conservatism, one can see many possibilities without posing a negation to any of these views as black. These views do not represent all Africanization of African Americans and they are not all views of the abdication of culture and history for African Americans, but these views, coming into play, in Fuller's mind are clearly African American characteristics, traits, and ethos. What Fuller is dealing with in the play are various attitudes and permutations of sensibilities that provide us comfort or discomfort depending upon our own historical consciousness. Who is invested in what view and who is insensitive to what condition might address our unease at some of the scenes. I like the fact that Fuller is not a man of polarities but one of nuances and his drama is always fluid. Yet Fuller's fluidity is not the lack of purpose and place but rather the ability to move between the convergences in human society.

Convergences are not the same as intersections, though one cannot get to an intersection without some sort of convergence when we happen upon an Eshuean point of decision. In the Yoruba culture Eshu is viewed as the one who controls the crossroads where everything converges. Once we are at the crossroads then we are in the vicinity of intersections. Until we are at the intersection we are merely on the way, that is, we are converging. But what Fuller underscores is the fact that in any human situation we are always moving in and out of intersections. Therefore, in his works he seeks to take one character close to another's in order to underscore the interaction like a puppeteer pulling the strings of both the characters' and the audiences' emotions. We know his characters because they are so well rounded in their emotional development. We see them mature and we often see them collapse.

Charles Fuller has a keen historical vision and this has put him in contact with the works of John Hope Franklin, Vincent Harding, W. E. B. Du Bois, Carter G. Woodson, St. Clair Drake, and other major historians of the African American community. One cannot navigate the dramatic waters of African American history without understanding the twists and turns of culture, customs, and traditions. The commonality between Fuller and the historians is one of unique perspective on facts; indeed, one might say the similarity of a common quest as well. The historians want the facts and Fuller wants the display of a variety of emotions based on the facts whether invented out of real materials or imagined on the basis of historical consciousness. These are always ideas on the edge of literary revolt and transgression because blacks were often not considered subjects of centered, agency-laden, ideas. But there is no dramatic fury here, only a slight nod to the ideology of humanity.

I do not forget that Frantz Fanon's *The Wretched of the Earth* must have impacted Charles Fuller as much as it had impacted his childhood friend Larry Neal. Although Neal was born in Atlanta he grew up in Philadelphia and lived four doors from Fuller in the same public housing projects. They both attended St. Elizabeth Elementary School and graduated from Roman Catholic High

School. Although Neal was two years older than Fuller, they became lifelong best friends. They were both interested in literature and culture. They became known as the two radical playwrights of Philadelphia in the 1960s and 1970s. Neal attended Lincoln University and the University of Pennsylvania, receiving a Bachelors and a Master's degree, respectively. He went off to New York to teach at City College for a year and then on to Wesleyan University, in a sense riding the wave of black consciousness that had gripped the nation. Neal taught at Yale for five years from 1970 to 1975. Although Neal worked with Amiri Baraka and several other writers in forming the Blacks Arts Repertory theatre, establishing the Black Arts Movement, and creating defining standards for art during the Black Power Movement it is his collaboration with Charles Fuller in Philadelphia that made its impact on his work in New York. Like Fuller, Larry Neal wrote for the *Liberator* and several local magazines and journals, and sought to enhance the meaning of African American letters for his compatriots. In fact, Neal directed two plays of a four-play cycle, "My Many Names and Days," written by Fuller and produced by Woodie King at the New Federal Theatre in the 1970s. Neal died in 1981 just a year before his friend Charles Fuller received the Pulitzer Prize.

Both Fuller and Neal understood the intricate nature of the weave that hung on the American tree. Fanon knew that the burden of colonialism, racism, and white hegemony as expressed in the French assault on the Algerians or Martinicans or Guadeloupeans was a price that had to be paid by all black people who lived in the West. As George Elliot Clarke, the Canadian novelist once asked, "Can you believe that Barack Obama also read Fanon's *The Wretched of the Earth?*" Fuller's reading leads him to action in his drama and Obama's reading remains a theoretical abstraction. There was an admission in Fuller's construction of A Soldier's Play that racism was rampant, that an arrogant construction of society in which racial, not merely ethnic, but racial representation mattered to Americans. I see in this recognition no canonical adherence to some black nationalist or integrationist ideology but as I have said a fierce adoption of a stance toward humanity with all of the contradictions and oddities that we possess as humans. Does this awareness reduce the Fullerian quest for a new type of response to human complexity? No, it does not create loss; it rather allows us to gain width and depth at another level of clarity in our relationships with each other. However, as we see in the dramatic tension between the characters this has to be achieved among Africans as well as between blacks and whites.

Thus, if Fuller is interested in anything aesthetic here, and I believe he is; then it has to be the use of a creative imagination to think afresh about the human condition by arguing, I say this with some apprehension, for a valid multidimensionality that is the core of African American identity. One can say that it was not always the case, say, when we first came ashore in Virginia in 1619, but then we do not know what arguments, contentions, and tensions existed among the twenty Africans who saw the English colony for the first time. Do we?

As we take a look at *A Soldier's Play* from another angle, and there are a myriad of angles that one can use to examine, critique, and learn from a play as profound as *A Soldier's Play*. Indeed, the Afrocentric scholar Ama Mazama, who like Fanon and Cesaire hails from the French Antilles, speaks of various categories of black responses to the existential condition of living in a racist society. One such condition or response is that of the *malevolent Negro* who works to make life hard for other blacks. Her categorization of "types of negroes" seeks to clarify the variety of African responses to living in societies where the doctrine of white superiority is promoted. Those societies are evidences of complex behaviors and sometime warped reactions to each other.

Fuller creates a space for negotiating our fears and our wishes of what could be by giving us a dramatic play about existence and choices. There is an Eshuean quality to *A Soldier's Play* because everything depends upon decision. Decision is perhaps the only authentic response to the existential situation that these black soldiers find themselves at their army base. Of course, a critic might question whether or not Fuller's militant is in fact an authentic nationalist militant in the tradition of Alexander Crummell, Martin Delany, and Marcus Garvey meaning that the character is the type of black person who understands precisely why self-hatred has to be placed in a proper historical context. Fuller's idea seems to be to that art, especially literature, is only one slice of life and no playwright can be required to present all the possible human possibilities but must be honest in his or her portrayals of the possibilities presented. This is another way of saying that the stage is only one reality and it might not be the core reality that we are living at any given time. I remember that the black literati made a lot of whoopee about the debate between Fuller and Baraka, but there was no debate and Fuller did not participate in the trashing of Baraka. I think that he understood the political and literary context of Baraka's criticism. Baraka had been a much more prolific playwright and had participated in the bohemian Greenwich Village scene and the cultural nationalist movement as a writer and activist. In some respects Baraka was thought by some to be the natural inheritor of the mantle of James Baldwin and Richard Wright and yet here comes Charles Fuller from North Philadelphia, a working intellectual, a serious literary reader, a consummate dramatist, and a compatriot of Larry Neal's, the same Larry Neal embraced by Amiri Baraka for his brilliance, to capture the Pulitzer Prize. One could say that some of the criticism of Fuller by other writers may have been provoked by the feeling that Fuller had not paid the same dues that the "militant" writers in Baraka's school, such as Haki Madhubuti, Sonia Sanchez, and others had paid. It is hard to say this for a fact because no one has been so crass as to express this sense of personal envy. However, the fact that a few writers had the courage to publicly applaud Fuller was a remarkable testimony to their integrity.

Icons and Text

Writing anything in a serious vein is difficult work and the best writers know this very well. One of the keys Charles Fuller often employs is the icon. What I mean by the icon is not some religious relic or sacred talisman but the intellectual marker for a particular society, group, and nation at a given time in history. Well, Charles Fuller is among the best writers in this tradition and that is why he remains a dramatic original. To master this technique one has to be well-read, creative, and capable of amassing a lot of information and making sense out of it.

I think that Fuller used every conceivable bit of his experience to craft *A Soldier's Play* whether it was friendships, art, athletics, hearsay, philosophy, printing, music, or other artists. This is the preeminence of the aggressive mind in search of ordering icons that would guide the spectator and, in some cases, the reader toward a close understanding of the play but also an appreciation of the dramatist's gift. When this is done effortlessly, as it is in Fuller's drama, it is seen as one of the marks of genius.

A Soldier's Play is dedicated to Larry Neal in memory of his heroic qualities as an activist writer and his aesthetic urges based upon the things black people did. Thus, Neal is himself an iconic marker for this play because he was so deeply appreciative of Fuller's genius as Fuller was of his. When one enters the play itself several significant icons strike the intelligent reader as leading aspects of Fuller's quest to educate the audience, as we are entertained.

Fuller's composition of *A Soldier's Play* finds a strong measure of contextual history in the narrative of baseball. Black baseball was special. The soldiers had a particularly keen attachment to the American Game that had become by the 1940s the official African American Game. In fact, one of Fuller's uncles played for the Grays. Giants walked the land like kings and their names may have been Satchel Paige, Josh Gibson, Cool Papa Bell, Norman "Turkey" Stearns, George "Mule" Suttles, Jimmie Crutchfield, Pop "El Cuchara" Lloyd, and Oscar Charleston. There was no question in the minds of black people, and some whites, that black baseball was the home to some of the greatest players of the game had ever seen. There were hitters like Josh Gibson, sometimes called the greatest baseball hitter of all time, but Gibson did not standalone. Men with names like Stuart Slim Jones, Dick Lundy, John Beckwith, Dobie Moore, Sam and Dan Bankhead, Chet Brewer, Buck O'Neill, Satchel Paige, Wild Bill Wright, Piper Davis, Walter McCoy were right besides the indefatigable Josh Gibson.

So when the United States finally decided to go to war against the National Socialists of Germany in 1941 some black players went to the army and played baseball. Jackie Robinson and Bullet Rogan played on the military teams but also went on to play for the Negro Leagues. Some players like Robinson, Roy Campanella, and Hank Aaron, would go on to become superstars in the major league. Black communities came out by the thousands to see their heroes play the Game. The Kansas City Monarchs controlled the western boundary of the game but the teams stretched clear across the nation to Boston and Atlantic City. Popular entertainers like Bill Bojangles Robinson, Joe and Marva Louis, Louis Armstrong, Lena Horne, and Billie Holiday would find their way to the ball parks to see the black stars play. No wonder Fuller weaves the baseball subtext into his play. It demonstrates social intelligence as well as an intimate relationship with the Americanization of the African and the Africanization of the American Game not even one hundred years after the Civil War.

One recalls that in *A Soldier's Play*, Davenport asked Wilkie, "How long did you know Sergeant Waters?" Wilkie's response was "bout a year, sir." Then he goes on a long description of the context of his experiences with the sergeant. At this point Wilkie says "This company was basically a baseball team then, sir. You see most of the boys had played for the Negro League." Wilkie talks about how C. J. Memphis could hit a ball "from Fort Neal to Berlin, Germany or Tokyo." From this point in the play Fuller uses the subtext of the team, (the baseball team), as a cultural icon understood to have been a major part of the leisure life of blacks in the 1940s. Basketball had not yet gained entry into the ambition of the young African American male. Every city of any size, say 20,000 people, had a baseball team that was attached to a league. It would not be until the 1950s and 1960s that Negro League baseball would suffer its most severe economic blows and become unsustainable because of the integration of the white leagues. Fuller's organization of this iconic piece of African American life fits neatly into his construction of the role of informal activities in the midst of a serious inquiry into murder.

The way I see Fuller's construction is that it is neither rigid nor fluid, but rather a portrait, a singular portrait, of African American dilemmas over the issues of humanity, culpability, suspicion, and race. We have not resolved these aspects of the American society and we could not expect a playwright in one play to answer all of our issues, but what we have in this dynamic work is the intertwining of the familiar with the unexpected. Drawing upon his knowledge of the African American culture and its complex history, Fuller indicates an awareness of Hughes, Wright, Ellison, Baldwin, Morrison, as he has his characters reveal the many quests that have occupied African American writers.

Fuller gives deference to the ideas that have gone before his own. This is one mark of a literary genius. At once, after reading or seeing the first section of the play one can understand that the general notion of an arrogant sense of aesthetic authenticity is foreign to Fuller's drawing of his characters. This has to be said because there is no canonical purity created by some hegemonic ideas of authenticity. Take his cut on music, for example; that is, the way he understands and presents a view of African Americans and the musical idiom. Who are the musicians and what is the music that comes front-and-center in this play? Like baseball, the blues were the essence of the Black South in the 1940s.

Blues could be heard every day somewhere coming from the two room shotgun houses that lined the dirt roads of Louisiana, Alabama, Georgia, South Carolina and Mississippi. This is the richness that Fuller tapped into when he layered the play with motifs of music that were endemic to the black community. No other music could accompany his play with such brilliance and originality as the blues. Son House, Henry Sims, and Blind Willie Reynolds were just a few of the giants who stood on the stages of the South and delivered the sad and often tragic news of the disappointments, failures, killings, and bad debts that followed black life around the American South. Thus when Sergeant Vernon C. Waters is killed in April 1944 in Tynin, Louisiana at Fort Neal, a black military camp, there was nothing to do but call forth the blues. Charles Fuller knew this context so well that he has the blues layered throughout the text and when the play is seen one never loses sight of the power of the people's song and the charisma that accompanied the singer of the music.

Joe Louis had conquered the heavyweight division of boxing a few years before 1944 so Fuller takes full advantage of another icon of black soldiers. In fact, Private James Wilkie tells Captain Richard Davenport that he is from the same town, "born and raised" where Joe Louis became a professional boxer. Louis may have been born in the South but he called Detroit his home. The idea that an African American could dominate the heavyweight division during a time when Jack Johnson had become a distant memory to some people was electrifying to most blacks of the 1940s. Joe Louis served his time in the army as well and became even more of an icon, not just for blacks but also for whites as well.

An iconic aspect often used in black theatre that one does not see in Fuller's construction is lots of religion. If one thinks of James Baldwin, for example, one thinks of the church experiences. In fact, *Amen Corner*, Baldwin's most memorable play makes religion and the church service keys to understanding the contradictions in black life. Fuller has none of this because he is aware that the life experiences of black people are far more than religion. It is just one aspect of the life of Africans.

One must ask, however, does Fuller run away from religion? Why is it that Fuller rejects the trope of African American religion found in so many dramas? His characters are not anti-religion they are just oblivious to it. I think that Fuller associates the African tradition to the past, especially the distant past, that is, the past that transcends and precedes the slavery past. Some could choose to see this as a methodological move toward a genetic orientation. I chose to see it as an acceptance of the inadequacy of religion to really transform the black communities because religion itself is a system of slavery. One cannot leap from the entanglements of religious rules with their prohibitions and the spectra of punishment to a reality of freedom without an evolved sense of self. Fuller recognizes this and while he uses the religious motif lightly he does not render his dramas as religious plays. There is no sense of James Baldwin's *"Amen Corner"* in Fuller. He has a different perspective on the nature and importance of religion in the lives of black people and his work seeks to march toward a rational place rather than an irrational one. I do not mean this in a negative manner, but as an observation of the critical difference between the icons chosen by different authors. Furthermore, there is no sense that this is timeless or unchanging; one never knows what an author will do with his next play, novel, or essay.

Perhaps nothing explains Fuller's creative genius more than his engagement with an inter-textuality between human and human as he seeks to destroy both the glorification and the beastification of the African. He does not begin this process from the syncretism of African traditions as say Toni Morrison might or from am epic of the African's covenant with the Middle Passage as an Afrocentrist might, but rather from an attempt to unlock the tragic consciousness of the African in order to be able to see into the room of humanity. To say this is not to say that he is dis-consonant with the narrative of African origin, myths, languages, customs, traditions, and heritages, but rather to say that Fuller is preeminently an explicit master of the historical moment. He uses juxtaposition as a driving semantic and dramatic force to trace what we know about African American culture.

The real motive of Fuller's drama is emancipation. He shows a modernist impulse in this regard because for him his drama is not resigned to devouring freedom but rather is revealing of a position on affirmation of culture and the criticism of anti-cultural behavior and action almost as a resistance to the destruction of black culture. I call this a modernist impulse only because I see Fuller presenting the African American culture with a sustained yet energetic reflection on our history. *A Soldier's Play* is a play about history but also a reflection on the future. He perceptively understands the anguish and pain of being black in a white world even when you are in the midst of other black people. The soldiers are not surrounded everyday by white people but they are acutely aware of their social and psychological context. I do not recall any verbal or should I say mental flagellation as severe as that which captures Sgt. Waters in his complicated relationship with a young private whose love for his culture is worn bravely in his every action. Sgt. Waters represents so many African Americans who when confronted by the overwhelming awareness of hatred toward blacks turn toward self-disdain and the hatred of anyone who appears to look or act black. There is a didactic honesty in the play that is instructive for the viewer and any other person who seeks to appreciate the enigmatic relationship we can have with each other in an insane asylum of a nation.

Fuller's brilliant opening with the shooting death of Sgt. Waters establishes the foundation upon which he builds the entire drama. Conveying the possibility that Waters could have been killed by a white man or a black man allows Fuller to toy with our loves and hates, our fears and wishes, and to thrust us headlong into the fray as we take sides in the play.

Fuller uses flashbacks to show what Waters was really like as an officer. We see the full range of his disdain for black men and the culture they expressed. He was light-skinned, very intelligent, and exceedingly ambitious as an officer. He felt that blacks could hold him back; indeed, he felt that the behavior of certain African Americans could create problems for him and for themselves. He loathed their love of music, social humor, and spirituality. To Waters these attitudes and behaviors spoke to old-fashioned stereotypes. He wanted to send his children to elite schools, and he wanted them to associate with whites because he saw blacks as "Uncle Toms and lazy, shiftless Negroes." He wanted to be as far away from these types of blacks as he could be. He especially hated Private C. J. Memphis because of his humor, jive-talking, and love of black music. Private Memphis was just the type of black man that reflected badly on the race and made it difficult for people like Sgt. Waters to succeed. Waters had to rid the earth of Memphis. His harassment, brutality, and vindictiveness caused Memphis to hang himself. The rest of the men saw the suicide as being caused by Sgt. Waters' attitude against Private Memphis. There was nothing that could save Waters from the hatred that his men felt for him. They loved Private Memphis, and hence, their culture and they saw in Sgt. Waters the tragic figure of the black man who had internalized the self-hatred of one who is trapped by the white racist superstructure.

Like someone who gets an epiphany just before he is killed, Sgt. Waters apparently came to realize that no matter what you do, no matter how much you try to be like whites, no matter how much you hate your own people, and no matter how much you despise yourself, "they still hate you." The realization comes too late for Sgt. Waters. Yet in some ways this last enigma opens the door to a further crinkle in the play because one is to ask, "Who is the "they" in this sentence?" Ostensibly it refers to the whites and one can leave it at that as the play proceeds but certainly Fuller is clever enough to leave us with the possibility that hatred could have come from any place. I think that Fuller's characters have so much breadth and depth that he appeals to blacks and whites with an equanimity that is rare among contemporary playwrights. The implication of both in the murder of Sgt. Waters without patronizing either is at the core of the deftness of his structure.

Waters' death like that of Private Memphis is a tragic death; these were deaths that did not have to happen except for the brazen horror of the white supremacist system. I see clearly what Fuller is up to in this play and find it strange that the play generated some negative heat when it first opened. The cast of the opening performance was magnificent. The play, directed by Douglas Turner Ward, was staged by the Negro Ensemble Company at the Lucille Lortel Theatre in Greenwich Village on November 10, 1981; it did not end until 468 performances later, making it one of the longest running plays by an African American playwright. It won the Pulitzer Prize but also the Outer Critics Circle Award for Best Off-Broadway Play, the New York Drama Critic's Award for Best

American Play, and the Obie Award for Distinguished Ensemble Performance. The original cast included outstanding performances by Adolph Caesar as Sergeant Waters, Denzel Washington as Private Peterson, Larry B. Riley as Private C.J. Memphis, Samuel L. Jackson as Private Louis Henson, and Peter Friedman as Captain Charles Taylor.

CHAPTER SIX

The Theatre of Being Black

Everyone seems to know about black people, but unfortunately this knowledge is an illusion, even for many black people. In fact, what they know is often stereotypical, and that hinders complete appreciation for the fullness of the African experience. There are avenues to know in the rhythms of the ordinary people and in the music of those who sing from the heart that run in myriad directions. Nothing proceeds in a straight line. This is what Fuller knew from his understanding of the Blues, Jazz, Gospel, and even the Spirituals. Nothing could be any more authentic to the black person than song, music, and telling the narratives of pain and suffering through comedy and drama. I think one of the reasons *A Soldier's Play* resonated with the masses that experience it is the fact that it is genuine in its portrayal of blacks interacting around the challenges of identity, culture, murder, and guilt. Fuller knew not only the character of black people but the character of whites as well. All illusions about humans evaporate when confronted with the possibilities in life. It is simple to proclaim the sacrosanct position of a black purity of purpose and a virtuous attitude toward other humans when you limit the possibility of humanity. Just as the American founding fathers proclaimed their own liberty while enslaving African masses by the hundreds of thousands at the time, so it is with those who proclaim the brutal capability of the white man but who believe that to demonstrate black guile, deceit, and murder is an anathema.

Fuller's genius in *A Soldier's Play* conquers all fears of misunderstanding. The idea is clear, cogent, and remarkably classic.[1] Those who rushed to criticize the play from their narrow havens of human interest only prolonged the possibility of their salvation from a disoriented examination of the play. The argument that the murderer should have been a white man misses the point of the play. The whites who were murdering blacks in the South had racial animosity at the top of their reasons; Waters' killer attacked him because he considered him a bully. The whites that lynched blacks in the South were themselves the bullies; they were the culprits of caprice, wanton murder, and insane racism. Indeed Fuller has a telling scene in the play about Waters' interaction with two white soldiers. When Davenport questions Taylor about what the two white soldiers had told him about their interaction with Waters, this is what happened. The two whites, Byrd and Wilcox, were coming off bivouac when they saw Waters outside the club. Waters walked toward them and said, "Well, if it ain't the white boys!" The white soldiers tell Taylor that it was not that they were looking for trouble but that Waters brought trouble to them. Waters addressed the white soldiers: "White boys! All starched and stiff! Wanted everybody to learn all that symphony shit! That's what you were saying in France—-and you know, I listened to you? Am I all right now? Am I?" Fuller demonstrates Waters' severe mental stress because he wanted so much to be like those who had punished him and yet they rejected him. He followed their admonitions, walked in step with their demands, and yet he was not good enough. One of the white soldiers said to Waters: "Boy, you'd better straighten up and salute when you see an officer, or you'll find yourself without those stripes!" Waters reject the white officers' command to salute and straighten up. He tells them that he is through "straightenin' up" for white folks. "I ain't doin' nothin' white folks say do, no more!" Waters has had it with this life of trying to fit into the white formula for black acceptance. Byrd shoves Waters in the face and soon Wilcox is restraining Byrd. All the while Waters is having a cathartic oration about how hard he has tried to follow what he was taught about being a good citizen. His daddy told him how to talk, where to live, and how to act so that whites would accept him and still whites reject him. The fact that he is intoxicated makes his statements more authentic because they reveal his hidden thoughts, emotions, and resentments. He is exhausted that he has tried everything and yet whites see him as a black man. Wilcox pleads with Byrd to leave Waters alone because "he's sick." Nothing more rational has ever been said about blacks that run away from their own culture and history. Sickness among black people results in the lack of self-definition. Fuller's dramatic display of a theatre of authentic human being subjects us to a rational universe where we are able to see, especially in *A Soldier's Play*, the varieties of our illnesses.

Fuller never relinquishes his authority to describe the contexts and environments of his drama; this is something he refuses to give up completely to any director. In *Zooman and the Sign,* for example, Fuller describes the setting of the play as consisting of three distinct locations: the living room of the Tate house, which is middle-class, modern, and well furnished, with a staircase leading upstairs and an exit to the kitchen; a front stoop; and a more abstract area for Zooman, which is described as "a raised platform where the actor should be able to pace". This is a telling description because the idea behind "pacing" is deeply grounded in the imagery of reflection, perhaps even worry, but certainly the pain of trying to come to terms with something profoundly disturbing in one's life or society. The pacing attitude is an attitude of apprehension where the character must consider his actions, his purposes, and his end. What will he do, say, or how will he behave in a given circumstance? Fuller insists that there be this pacing space on the raised platform. Even the raised platform is something Fullerian because to describe the space for Zooman in this way is to demonstrate that the character should be "up there" for all people to see.

I recall as a young boy sitting in a church in South Georgia when the preacher at our little church spoke about Jesus and the woman who had been caught in adultery. Stoning was to be the punishment for this act. He had called upon the person without sin to cast the first stone and when he looked up all of the men had slipped away. Then Jesus told the woman, "Go and sin no more." I had always looked to this parable as a strong indication that we are all guilty of something and that we were all in need of some kind of understanding. This is not to accept the deeds of Zooman but rather to see his deeds and ours as forming some interactive discourse about the lousy nature of our fraternity with each other. Neighbors who refuse to act are just as guilty as the lone culprit who threatens the order of our society.

Fuller also characterizes the sign itself in *Zooman*. The sign in the play title appears at the end of Act I; it literally shouts that the neighbors saw the murder of the Tate's daughter Jinny but were to cowardly to identify the killers. When the play was first produced the sign existed in two forms: a real sign placed outside by Jinny's father and a larger projection of the sign on panels which closed in front of the living room. When Zooman is shot at the end of the play, he destroys Jinny's sign; and there is a new sign which tells the audience Zooman's real name and says that he will be missed by family and friends.

I had read Zooman several times before I saw the production in New York in 2009. In that production I could feel Fuller's insistence that we, the audience, get involved in saving our own communities. When Zooman says, "What am I doing here now? I just killed somebody. A Little girl, I think," the disintegration of the community's code of values or continuing lack of values reaches us with immediacy. This call to awareness is naked, unclothed in any fancy words, point blank, direct. It is this drive that pushes us out of apathy about the conditions in our neighborhoods and causes a strong reaction to fear and apprehension.

A dramatist cannot be all things, for example, Fuller is neither a sociologist nor a psychologist, but he is a master at drama. However, the character of Zooman tells us a lot about what is going on but we do not get to learn the origin of Zooman's value deterioration. We do not know who caused him to lose his way? We do not know how he was forced or allowed himself to be pushed into a world of decadence.

Fuller's Zooman asks, "Why am I the way I am?" In fact, this is an existential question that is laid at the door of everyone in the audience. Do you know, for example, why you are the way you are? Is it fair to have Zooman raise this question? Would someone like Zooman even realize how to answer this question, how to approach it. How many times have we seen people in our own communities, perhaps our own relatives, avoid dealing with that question because they do not know who they are as individuals or collectively as members of a cultural or ethnic group with deep historical ties to the movement of humans. We are who we say we are and who we act like we are; we cannot be any better than what we do. "A child ain't supposed to be out on that stoop in the middle of the night," Zooman says about the young girl he kills. He challenges the audiences to accept its own responsibility for the plight of our youth and our neighborhood. What Zooman knows, because Fuller fills him with this sense, is that family is important but that the structure of all families is fragile given the inability of modern urban dwellers to control the entire environment. Living in Philadelphia or Chicago is different from living in some small village. We are touched by the interactions in the family, split apart by the emotions, cramped in our ability to speak when we see the demise of sanity, and shocked at our inability to act in the face of the overwhelming requirement to be decent, ethical, and proactive. Who can heal us if not ourselves? Who can save us from apathy if not our own action? What is the requirement of moral outrage if it is not the protection of our family, our own neighborhood, and our children? Fuller knows and believes that we have the capacity to rise to the front of the line in defense of our most treasured human values, but we are damaged, bent, and in some cases broken. It might be that we are as broken as Zooman himself who can never rise to the position of leader in the community because of the pressure to commit havoc. What potential resides in the body and mind of a young man who is a warrior and one who is ready to fight for the wrong things? Suppose, just suppose we have a different reality where speaking one's mind, acting in one's interest, and establishing a djed, place, where one can make a moral stand is acceptable within the context of our society? Who is to say then that Zooman's end is inevitable? We are culpable as a society in this anti-individualistic play. Fuller does not allow us to hide behind our unique individualism though he does not deny that there are unique features to our personalities and histories, but ultimately we are all partakers and participants in this drama where our values are *renditioned*, much like during the Iraqi War, until such time as they are permitted to advance as valid commentaries on our lives. We chastise ourselves because we know that what our children are doing is not what they should be doing. Somebody should have stopped Zooman a long time ago. Indeed we have also abdicated our own position and stepped back from the decisions that we should make about getting Zooman off of the street.

The play is therapeutic for those of us who seek to transform the community and therefore it is not unknown or uncommon for people to shed tears when they see the play. They react to it as a testament to the chaos that occurs in some of the neighborhoods in large cities. Memory is a powerful weapon and the people who experience the everyday grind of crime statistics and the reality of youth deaths know that they must be the keepers of the society. *Zooman and the Sign* has become a classic in the genre of cathartic plays. We are all affected by its meaning and strength because it strikes at the heart of existential reality in America.

Zooman says, "If you don't deal with me now, you'll deal with me later." This is a proven truth and over and over again we see it in the condition of our lives. But it is first of all a family condition, that is, a situation where parents or guardians who do not train, educate, advise, and control their children will have to deal with them at another level when they are older and perhaps in much more serious situations. At a community level we have to tackle the issues of violence, disorder, and chaos at a macro-level as well as at the family level. I mean Fuller knows that the society itself is responsible for much of the social disease that exists. If there are guns in our community that we cannot regulate, politicians who are corrupt, preachers who take advantage of children, or malaise, anomie, and apathy in the face of constant decay in our neighborhoods then we are confronted with a most direct moral crisis that can only be answered by African Americans. It is not for us to throw up our hands and say that we cannot influence the arts, politics, social activities, and education in the urban environment. Our survival as a community depends, if anything, on us, that is, our own will to act in the interest of our safety and our security.

Almost no modern African American dramatist, and there are some very good playwrights, understands intuitively the historical relationship to the succedaneum of the African gods and *orishas* as Charles Fuller. This is why we have Crisis, Beauty, Evil, War, Envy, Shame, and Honor in abundance in Fuller's works.

When the Zooman comes out at night we must not go inside and shut our door but we must be actively engaged in confronting what the ancient Egyptians called *isfet*, evil. This is what the dead girl's father understood. One must fight against evil because the person committing the evil act might want to deflect responsibility and claim that the society is the problem. Yet the decent people of a community must see clearly the reason for standing up against all forms of chaos. *Isfet* was written in the ancient ciKam as a symbol of a man splitting his own head with an ax. Those who operate in the shadows on the margins of reason and ethics must be brought into the light. Fuller knows, because I have asked him, that the people who should be in the theater are people like Zooman. But how do you take the theater into the neighborhoods in disarray? What mechanisms have we established in our communities to break through the reluctance to engage?

Zooman is a play that pursues us to our very moral core. It challenges our inability or reluctance to act in the face of utter chaos. Yet we know that there is a reality on the other side of the chaos but we must be brave enough, that is, have enough courage to encounter our own weaknesses and unite in common cause against the Zooman factor. As Marcus Garvey would have asked, "Can we do it?" The answer is, yes, we can do it because no one will do it for us. Fuller sees that we are permanently on our own and must be shown to take responsibility for our actions and our inactions. No one can deny the fact that we encounter everyday challenges to our conceptions of truth, justice, righteousness, harmony, order, balance, and reciprocity; ideas that ancient Africans considered to be as old as the cosmic origin of the universe.

Charles Fuller's Works

The Village: A Party, Princeton, N.J., McCarter Theater, November 1968; produced as *The Perfect Party,* New York: Tambellini's Gate Theater, 20 March 1969.

Sunflower Majorette and *Untitled Play*: Two New One Act Plays, December 16-19,1970

In My Many Names and Days, first produced in New York: New Federal Theatre, September 1972.

The Candidate, first produced in New York: New Federal Theatre, April 1974.

In the Deepest Part of Sleep, first produced in New York by the Negro Ensemble Company: St. Marks Playhouse, 4 June 1974.

First Love (one-act), first produced in New York: Billie Holiday Theatre, June 1974.

The Lay out Letter (one-act), first produced in Philadelphia: Freedom Theatre, Spring 1975.

The Brownsville Raid, first produced in New York: Theater DeLys, 5 December 1976.

Zooman and the Sign, first produced in New York by the Negro Ensemble Company: New York: Samuel French, 1982.

A Soldier's Play, first produced in New York by the Negro Ensemble Company: New York: Hill and Wang, 1982

We, first produced in New York by the Negro Ensemble Company, Theatre Four, 1988

Eliot's Coming, first produced in New York City, 1988.

Snatch: The Adventures of David and Me in Old New York, a novel, Philadelphia: David and Me, 2010.

Commentaries on Charles Fuller

Anadolu-Okur, Nilgun. *Contemporary African American Theater: Afrocentricity in the Works of Larry Neal, Amiri Baraka, and Charles Fuller.* New York: Garland, 1997.

Baraka, Amiri. "The Descent of Charlie Fuller into Pulitzerland and the Need for African American Institutions." *Black American Literature Forum* (Summer, 1983): 51-4.

Harriot, Esther. *American Voices: Five Contemporary Playwrights in Essays and Interviews.* Jefferson, NC: McFarland and Company, 1988.

"Charles (H. Jr.) Fuller." *The Gale Literary Database: Contemporary Authors Online.* 15 Nov. 2005. 12 Mar. 2006. <http://www.galenet.galegroup.com>.

Rich, Frank. "Stage: Negro Ensemble Presents 'A Soldier's Play.'" *New York Times* 27 Nov. 1981:

Charles Fuller's Movie and Television Credits

"The Sky is Gray" for television, (1980)

"A Soldier's Story," feature film, Columbia Pictures, 1984

"A Gathering of Old Men" (1987) (TV) ... aka *Aufstand alter Männer, Ein* (West Germany) ... aka *Murder on the Bayou*

"Zooman," Showtime Network, 1995

"Love Songs," Showtime Network, 1998

"The Badge," a segment written for "The Wall," on television, 1998

Memorable Cast of
A Soldier's Story

Howard E. Rollins Jr.	Capt. Davenport
Adolph Caesar	Sgt. Waters
Art Evans	Pvt. Wilkie
David Alan Grier	Cpl. Cobb
David Harris	Pvt. Smalls
Dennis Lipscomb	Capt. Taylor
Larry Riley	C.J. Memphis
Robert Townsend	Cpl. Ellis
Denzel Washington	Pfc. Peterson
William Allen Young	Pvt. Henson
Patti LaBelle	Big Mary
Wings Hauser	Lt. Byrd
Scott Paulin	Capt. Wilcox
John Hancock	Sgt. Washington
Trey Wilson	Col. Nivens

Endnotes

Chapter One

1. The Black Revolution included the influences of the Civil Rights Movement, the Black Power Movement, and the Black Arts Movement, a period usually dated between 1954-1975. It involved the overturning of discriminatory segregationist laws as well as the assertion of a new, more authentic, African American sense of agency. Fuller's work has to be seen in the light of this intensely political and philosophical moment in American history.
2. Larry Neal's history was intertwined with that of Charles Fuller from the time they were in elementary school. By the time Larry Neal wrote in the *Ebony Magazine's* special issue on the Black Revolution he was thoroughly convinced that his young compatriot was one of the giants of Black Revolutionary consciousness and positioned Charles Fuller alongside Maya Angelou, Ed Bullins, Ron Milner, Jacob Lawrence, Eleo Pomare, and Aretha Franklin as artists who knew that political and economic responses to oppression were not enough. See *Black Revolution*, Chicago: Johnson Publishing Company, 1970, p. 50.

3. Gray, John. *Black Theatre and Performance: A Pan African Bibliography*. New York: Greenwood, 1990. One can easily study the arc of the black theatre by examining this fine bibliography.

4. Maya Asante says, "As an artivist, I contemplate global issues of war, poverty, waste, ageing and beauty; searching for what fuels our desire to preserve or protect. Giving reverence to my ancestors and meditating on the beauty of now, my artwork represents the freedom to create challenging work with an objective of universal peace and understanding. The peace starts with the community in which I'm sharing my work; interaction is ever present and essential." (http://www.mayafreelon.com/statement.html).

5. Lewis Gordon, the humanist philosopher, would later write *Existentia Africana: Understanding Africana Existential Thought* (Routledge, 2000) to underscore the idea that antiblack racism can be found in the yoking of reason to whiteness. Fuller sees antiblackness in the idea that blacks are devoid of passions, emotions, and actions that occur in others.

6. The Negro Ensemble Company was established in 1967 as a product of the turbulent Sixties by Douglas Turner Ward, Robert Hooks, and Gerald S. Krone. It would become one of the best incubators for African American playwrights and actors. Actors such as John Amos, Adolph

Caesar, Avery Brooks, Angela Bassett, Rosalind Cash, Laurence Fishburne, Al Freeman, Jr., Denzel Washington, Moses Gunn, Cleavon Little, Richard Rountree, Esther Rolle, Phylicia Rashad, and Antonio Fargas found a platform for their gifts at the NEC. Charles Fuller would become NEC's most successful playwright with the production of *A Soldier's Play*.

7. This play was reviewed by a number of writers. One can see a wide range of praise-singers and a single critic in the array of reviews presented here. Robert Asahina, A review of A Soldier's Play in *Hudson Review*, Vol. XXXV, No. 3, Autumn, 1982, pp. 439-42.

Baraka, Amiri. "The Descent of Charles Fuller into Pulitzerland and the Need for African-American institutions," in *Black American Literature Forum* Vol. 17, No. 2, Summer, 1983, pp. 51-54.

Clive Barnes, "A review of A Soldier's Play," in the *New York Post*, November 23, 1981.

Beaufort, John. "A Review of A Soldier's Play," in *The Christian Science Monitor*, December 1, 1981. While the play was not universally praised, it was considered a bold and daring dramatic project because the themes were authentic and appropriate and the story was compelling and real. Although Amiri Baraka's review appeared more inclined toward raising a political issue about who is to blame in the black community, Fuller's main point was that there was enough guilt to go around for everyone. I believe that Fuller dealt with this issue rightly by humanizing black people and moving blacks to the center of our own drama. He asks who is ultimately responsible for the situation. The answer is staring us in the face because of the deep necessity for accountability. Of course this is only one slice of life and in another situation we might be able to blame others, many others, but let us not excuse the African who has free will.

8. By saying this I am not claiming that Charles Fuller is a professional philosopher, but I am saying that his plays, although greatly entertaining, are always situated on the serious side of the art form. Fuller approaches drama with the gravitas of a reflective thinker while providing the audience with exciting stylistic and dialogic moments.

9. Wanda Macon *"Charles Fuller,"* in Linda Metzger, et. al., Berkeley: California: New Revision Series, 1990, pp. 206–208. Nothing in his biography seems to contradict his style and intelligence.

Chapter Two

1. May 2, 1982, *New York Times*.
2. Molefi Kete Asante, *Speaking My Mother's Language. Introduction to African American Language*. Fort Worth: Themba House, 2010. This work lays out the extent of language creation

and practice in the South Georgia communities out of which Fuller's family emerged to eventually land in Philadelphia.

3. What we know is that in the political realm the military is inviolable. In fact, the politician who attacks the military ceases to be a politician in any real sense in the United States; the nation is itself wrapped in the fabric of the military institution. Fuller realizes that the military is sacred and holy in the mind of many Americans, but he understands also that it occupies a major part of our imagination.

4. The entire debate over essentialism and situation has been argued in the universities but has almost no meaning to the people who struggle against what they see as situational racism based entirely upon blackness. Fuller's plays have limited meaning in the context of abstraction when in effect he is always seeking to humanize an irrational situation. So to say biology and culture is not to lure the prevalence of one over the other but to establish the point of situation as fundamental to how humans have reacted to other humans in the United States of America.

5. Maulana Karenga, *Maat: The Moral Ideal in Ancient Egypt*. Los Angeles: University of Sankore Press, 2006.

Chapter Three

1. The alienation of black people from their own language, clothes, ideas, concepts of good and beauty, and religion

creates a distance that comes through in almost every action of the characters in Fuller's plays.
2. Fuller demonstrates the undertones of the tension that exists in the society between blacks and the dominant white construction of reality. One knows as one reads his plays or experiences them as a spectator that they are reflective of the pressure points that activate genius.

Chapter Four

1. This remains a topic in the artistic community only because of the virulent attack on Fuller for winning the Pulitzer Prize. In no way was Fuller ever going to deny the black person his or her own humanity but preparing a corner for Africans to sit in as the world goes by. One has to compare the meaning of his drama with the criticism he gathered to see how he has handled these human issues in his plays. This is why I have written about his sincerity as a classic author.
2. Charles Fuller, interview, *New York Times,* May 2, 1982.
3. Amiri Baraka, "The Descent of Charlie Fuller into Pulitzerland and the Need for African American Institutions." *Black American Literature Forum,* (Summer, 1983): 51-54.
4. Nilgun Anadolu Okur, *Contemporary African American Theater: Afrocentricity in the Works of Larry Neal, Amiri Baraka, and Charles Fuller.* New York: Garland Press, 1997.

5. David Brotherton and Luis Barrios. *The Almighty Latin King and Queen Nation:Street Politics and the Transformation of a New York City Gang*. New York: Columbia University Press, 2004.
6. Lou Bellamy, *Zooman and the Sign* Study Guide, St. Paul, Minnesota: Penumbra Theatre, 2006.
7. David C. Brotherton and Luis Barrios, eds., *Gangs and Society: Alternative Perspectives*. New York: Columbia University Press, 2003. Fuller's play is one small piece on the general fabric of violence in the society. America is a violent place; its history has been woven in violent acts and the Zooman is an actor on the stage of America.

CHAPTER FIVE

1. See Charles Fuller, The Drexel Interview, Drexel News Bureau, July 19, 2007.
2. Lewis Gordon is one of the most brilliant philosophers of the 21st century and he has argued for the wisdom and knowledge inherent in the existential situation of the African person. See Gordon's *Existentia Africana: Understanding Africana Existential Thought*. New York: Routledge, 2000, for an in-depth treatment of the concept. He has written numerous books and articles on the subject. One could also read with interest his book, *Bad Faith and Antiblack Racism*, Amherst, NY: Humanity, 1995.

3. Frank Rich, "Negro Ensemble Presents 'Soldier's Play.'" *The New York Times*. November 27, 1981): 3.

4. Lou Bellamy started Penumbra in 1976 and guided it through its most important phase of production. Numerous other entrepreneurs of the theatre, some with artistic flair and skill, and others with simply a love of the theatre provided the space for the artists to mature. Bellamy's name rings loudly in the history of art in St. Paul.

Chapter Six

1. Walter Kerr, *"A Fine Work from a Forceful Playwright,"* New York Times, 6 December 1981, 3:1.